TRANSCULTURAL PERSPECTIVES IN THE HUMAN SERVICES

TRANSCULTURAL PERSPECTIVES IN THE HUMAN SERVICES
Organizational Issues and Trends

**ROOSEVELT WRIGHT, Jr.
Ph.D.**

*Associate Professor
Graduate School of Social Work
The University of Texas at Arlington
Arlington, Texas*

**DENNIS SALEEBEY
D.S.W.**

*Professor
Graduate School of Social Work
The University of Texas at Arlington
Arlington, Texas*

**THOMAS D. WATTS
D.S.W.**

*Associate Professor
Graduate School of Social Work
The University of Texas at Arlington
Arlington, Texas*

**PEDRO J. LECCA
Ph.D.**

*Professor
Graduate School of Social Work
The University of Texas at Arlington
Arlington, Texas*

CHARLES C THOMAS • PUBLISHER
Springfield • Illinois • U.S.A.

Published and Distributed Throughout the World by

CHARLES C THOMAS • PUBLISHER

2600 South First Street

Springfield, Illinois, 62717, U.S.A.

© *1983 by* CHARLES C THOMAS • PUBLISHER

ISBN 0-398-04737-5

Library of Congress Catalog Card Number: 82-10295

With THOMAS BOOKS *careful attention is given to all details of manufacturing and design. It is the Publisher's desire to present books that are satisfactory as to their physical qualities and artistic possibilities and appropriate for their particular use.* THOMAS BOOKS *will be true to those laws of quality that assure a good name and good will.*

Printed in the United States of America
CU-R-1

Library of Congress Cataloging in Publication Data

Main entry under title:

Transcultural perspectives in the human services.

　　Includes bibliographies and index.
　　1. Social work with minorities.　I. Wright,
Roosevelt.
HV3176.T72　1983　　　362.8′4　　　82-10295
ISBN 0-398-04737-5

DEDICATED TO

Elaine Wright
Bette Saleebey
Ilene Watts
Gina Lecca

the most important women in our lives

PREFACE

THE purpose of this book is to examine a transcultural perspective on the human services and the process of working within human service organizations with and on behalf of ethnic/racial minorities. Four areas of the human services have been chosen for special consideration: health and mental health services, income security services, family and child welfare services, and aging services. These areas have been chosen because they encompass the largest number of racial minorities that are currently served by human service organizations.

Organizations typically provide the context and vehicle for service delivery and practice. Human service organizations themselves are embedded in a larger social, cultural, and political milieu, and they tend to reflect the dominant ethics, perceptions, and assumptions of that milieu. A large number of the consumers of human services, however, do not share dominant perspectives; more often than not, these are ethnic minorities of color. Traditionally, friction, conflict, mistrust, and misinformation have characterized the relationship between human service organizations and these consumers.

It is an objective of this book to present a transcultural perspective which will —

a. provide an understanding of the viewpoints, problems and needs of ethnic minorities of color, particularly in certain service areas (child and family services, income security, mental health/health, and services to the aging)
b. clarify the nature of the conflict between the service organization and ethnic minority consumers
c. suggest the implications of a transcultural framework for organizational structure and process and human service practice
d. present proposals for change that will render human service organizations more responsive to their minority constituencies.

The first chapter provides both an introduction to the book as well as drawing the contours of what a comprehensive transcultural perspective on the human services might look like. The second chapter focuses on a transcultural perspective on income maintenance services, the third chapter is devoted to a transcultural perspective on aging services, and the fourth and fifth chapters are devoted to transcultural perspectives on health and mental health services and family and children services, respectively. The sixth and concluding chapter summarizes the previous chapters and draws some conclusions for conceptualizing and implementing a transcultural perspective on the human services.

This book should be looked at as a beginning set of statements on a complex subject. Research and scholarship still provide us with somewhat limited information and knowledge concerning a thorough understanding or implementation of a broad-ranging transcultural perspective on the human services. We would appear at this point to know slightly more about the psychology and sociology of minority groups and populations than we do about the services, policies, and organizations that impinge on the lives and well-being of minorities. It is instructive that organization theorists and researchers have not, on the whole, researched the effects of human service organizations on minorities as thoroughly as other areas. These are liabilities, which hopefully others following us will not have to experience, that our research has labored under. Still, much more research and thinking is available to us now on this seminal subject than ever before. This is fortunate, for a transcultural perspective is essential for the human service practitioner. Without it, he or she is doomed to continue to solidify the barriers between programs of service and the ethnic minorities of color who receive those services. Hopefully, this book will contribute in some small way to the elimination of those barriers.

The overall goal of this book is to provide to human service practioners different materials, resources, techniques, and ideas by which they may increase their knowledge and understanding of their own culture as well as that of others whom they serve. Ultimately, we recognize that practitioners, among others, will learn best about different cultural groups not from books or the advice of experts but from direct and meaningful contact with members of the groups. We hope, however, that this book will be the impetus that encourages practitioners to examine their own cultures and alternatives as they attempt to improve the quality of services given to ethnic minorities of color.

R.W., Jr.
D.S.
T.W.
P.L.

ACKNOWLEDGMENTS

WE would like to thank Ms. Billie Starr, librarian in the Multi-Ethnic Cultural Collection, The University of Texas at Arlington Library, for her assistance. We also would like to thank Ms. Judy Buckler, Joy Crow, and Cindy Viol for helping us in the final typing of the manuscript. We are dependent on all the scholarship and thinking that has gone before us on minorities and transcultural perspectives on the human services. A partial rendition of that scholarship to which we are jointly indebted is contained in the bibliographies at the end of each chapter. We are grateful for the support and encouragement of our families in this undertaking. Our lead author, Roosevelt Wright, kept us adhering to the necessary deadlines among other duties and his other contributions to the book. Dennis Saleebey laid down the transcultural model and groundwork, among other contributions. Finally, our thanks to all others who contributed in any way to helping pave the way for fruition of this book, especially the work of Madeline Leininger on transcultural nursing, work which considerably has leavened our own.

CONTENTS

TRANSCULTURAL PERSPECTIVES IN THE HUMAN SERVICES

Chapter 1

AN INTRODUCTION TO THE
TRANSCULTURAL PERSPECTIVE

E THNIC minorities of color make up a disproportionate share of the clientele of many human service agencies.[1] Reasons for this are abundant and include political, economic, and social inequality; barriers to the social resources (health care, special education, recreation and the like), which form the basis of personal, group, and family resourcefulness; institutionalized and personal racism; and the disharmonious clash of cultures and ideologies when minority and majority meet.[2] Oppressed by such inequities and barriers, when minorities seek assistance from human service agencies, they frequently encounter the same fractious and insensitive response from which they seek relief. One could lay the dissonance and disappointment of these encounters at the feet of racism, discrimination, and prejudice. There is ample justification for doing just that. However, it is the view of this book that a singularly important element in the friction of such encounters is cultural difference and, as a result, cultural conflict. Such conflict can be traced, in part, to differences in ideals, values, knowledge, and symbols rooted in the individual consciousness of all those partner to such exchanges. We would be foolish, of course, to ignore the complex relationship between culture and the politics and patterns of discrimination and racism. We will, however, in this book emphasize the cultural factor. Our rationale for doing this is simple. If, miraculously, institutionalized racism and organized discrimination were to vanish, the collective and individual relations between ethnic cultures or subcultures and the dominant culture in our society would continue to exude misunderstanding, defensive rigidity, and frustration.

What we propose, then, to accomplish in this book are the beginnings of a perspective to encourage human service organizations, practitioners, and students to become sensitive to the cultural barriers to understanding and service that thwart efforts to significantly

3

assist minority clientele. Before we introduce the makings of the perspective some basic assumptions are in order.

1. The ultimate value underlying the effort to enhance cross-cultural encounters in human service organizations is what Alice Rossi calls cultural integration.[3] Integration refers to the result of genuine, intense, egalitarian, and dialogic encounters between minority and majority; that the cultures will begin, in important ways, to merge and both will be different over time for the exchange. Integration is a hybrid. This doesn't mean that either culture must dissipate its unique elements, but it means that the consequences of free encounters will be synergistic — the end being different from the mere sum of the constituent parts. Intimate relationships of endurance and substance have this quality; each party changes as a result of the relationship, and both are different for it. The nature of their relationship is something idiosyncratically apart from the summation of their respective traits. Yet, each partner retains his/her individuality.

Another possible value is cultural pluralism. Here, ideally, each culture retains its uniqueness, and theoretically, each culture learns to respect and understand the other but also remains inured to changes that might result from mutual contact. The nobility of such a goal is unmistakable. The danger, however, is that one culture will continue to define the other's singularity in terms of available stereotypes, most of which are pernicious and have unwanted consequences. For example, Anglos will respect the quaint, though backward ways of Hispanic cultures, finding charm, say, in their imagined indolence. The upshot is the maintenance of the same kind of clumsiness and pain that now characterizes such relationships.

The least desirable ideal or value is the assimilative. A persistent goal of the dominant culture, assimilation essentially demands that "foreign" cultures or subcultures will finally melt into the cauldron of majority values, morals, and life-styles, and members of other cultures will emerge as black, brown, red, or yellow tintypes of the dominant culture. Boiled downs to its residue, assimilation means *culture killing*. Assimilation inevitably puts a variety of social pressures on minorities and creates shame about and humiliation over one's heritage.

Cultural integration does not presume the passing away of the minority culture but, rather, assumes that the conditions are open and free, and respectful contacts over time will create new cultural forms of which all will partake. An illustrative, though somewhat removed, example would be contacts between males and females. An integrative goal would mean that men and women both can be aggressive, nurturant, caring, and comfortable with reason and emotion and either dominant or submissive. Thus, those qualities that we value in the other become available to us as well, and the kinds of relationships we might have together cannot be predicted but unquestionably will be different, richer, and provide many more alternatives for self-realization and mutuality.

2. All cultures and subcultures are valid. There is no penultimate test of truth or verity. Every culture is an evolution of human beings' attempts — technical, symbolic, biological, and behavioral — to deal with the conditions of existence in general and the particular exigencies of a given group's geographical and temporal place. What in one culture crowns existence may in another debase it. Whose perspective is correct? Both. While we can make moral and ethical judgments about particular individual or collective behaviors of a people, we cannot make the same kind of judgment about their culture; it is they and they are it. To bury the placenta is no less valid than to throw it into a surgical bucket. And if cultural forms are believed and felt to be true by members of a given culture they are, in effect, true and should be so treated.[4]

3. There is a difference, conceptually and in reality, between race, ethnicity, and culture. The differences are not simple and clear. For purposes of this book ethnic groups will be so defined if they share a common sociohistory, have a sense of identity of themselves as a group, and have common geographical, religious, racial, and cultural roots. The central core of each ethnic group, welding it together with the thread of belief, styles of being, and adapting, is culture. Clearly, because of historical contact and intermingling, different ethnic groups share common cultural elements, and it would be nearly impossible to find an ethnic group unsullied by foreign cultures.

Race is, at this point, a dubious biological designation.[5] Unfortunately, though, it has signal social importance. People attach importance to it and frequently gauge their treatment of others on assumptions, usually mistaken, about race. Albert Murray once pointed out that in America we make clear distinctions between blacks and whites; the categories have an impact on how we think about and treat each other. From a biological and cultural stand-point he suggests that the truth is that we are an unmistakably mulatto culture. To accept such a belief, however, even if true, would upset a host of social artifacts, from social policies to informal relationships.[6] We have also referred to ethnic minorities of color, which is a loose designation at best. What we intend is the naming of Hispanic Americans, black Americans, native Americans, Asian Americans, Pacific Islanders, and Aleuts. Our specific concern in this book will be primarily Hispanic and black citizens.

A more extended definition of culture and subculture will come later in this chapter. For the moment, let it be said that culture provides the symbols by which we define and structure our reality. Culture runs deep within each of us, providing a force to negotiate our world. Shared assumptions, behavior patterns, values, tools, language, and beliefs are elements in our culture.[7] Without culture we, as animals, are naked in the world and vulnerable to its impersonal demands — no better off, perhaps, than feral children.

4. The failure of many social programs to meet the needs and help solve the problems of ethnic minorities of color turns important-ly on the ignorance of the reality and depth of cultural difference. Culture profoundly affects the way that people perceive and respond to threats to their psychosocial and physical existence; the symbolic meaning that people attach to these threats and the coping strategies adopted, individually and communally, are cultural products. To seek the services of a folk healer when one senses the malevolent workings of an enemy as the cause of illness is as adaptive in its way as submitting oneself to a $500 computerized physical examination. It must be remembered, however, that service agencies eminently represent the dominant culture. This is reflected in everything from their architecture to their policies to the demeanor with which they greet the new client. Paulo Friere's successful attempts to help cer-tain South American peasant groups help themselves (in spite of the political oppression, naked poverty, and rampant dispiritedness) always turned on the initial step of understanding the culture and its generative themes. To impose one's ideas on such groups, no matter how leavened by knowledge, experience, and expertise is, he thought, simply another form of oppression.[8]

5. Human service organizations and their practitioners would do well, if they are seriously interested in extending themselves to

minority communities and clientele, to take on a model of help substantially different from the professional, technical, or medical one they now employ. These models, which are close relatives of each other, reflect a number of dominant cultural ideas, which are, at times, seriously at odds with the way some groups think of their problems, troubles, and misfortunes. They also subvert the way some groups think of help or healing. The stance of this book is that organizations and individuals who want to help ethnic minorities of color can make their relationships more salutary by adopting some of the working assumptions of the diplomat or applied anthropologist. An elemental strategy is to understand the culture of the group they work with and to bridge the gap dug by cultural difference by building bridges to that culture. Whether the purpose is to merely understand, to render social or technical innovation, or to establish mutually beneficial relationships, the cultural language must be learned and the symbols of the culture respected for their validity. An applied anthropologist working as a consultant, say to a public health organization, would never presume that a medical or sanitary innovation introduced into a culture would be seen as good or wise by the people. There are powerful social, psychological, and cultural barriers to change. What looks to the outsider as an unmixed blessing may be the harbinger of disaster to the insider. So the applied anthropologist must understand the traditions, the language, the roles and the world views of the recipient population. We do not want to take this analogy too far, but we think it is a far safer and more productive one than usually directs the efforts of helpers and healers.[9]

6. The theoretical and practical knowledge that guides practice in human service organizations, widely regarded as ethically or culturally neutral, is probably not. It has risen from the cradle of culture and so bears its stamp. For example, much of the so-called theory that guides psychotherapeutic endeavors is an imaginative creation of white, middle-class males to be employed with white, middle-class females. When applied to groups from a dissimilar sociocultural background, such theory and its practices may flout the beliefs and behaviors of that group. Theories, like individuals and groups, may be sodden with ethnocentric bias. Yet, if we assume that the principles guiding human service practice are scientific, therefore universal and culturally neutral, we make the same mistake as the well-meaning public officials who assumed that

cooking stoves would be an unmitigated good and were abashed when the citizens of Zambia rejected them; the public health officials who knew that powdered milk was a nutritional necessity in Venezuela, only to have their faith in that nutritional good shaken by the cultural meaning of mother's milk; or officials in west Boston who knew that public urban renewal would be an unblemished benefit, only to see the citizens rise in protest of such an idea.[10] The anthropologist would know that, in each case, the innovation struck at some vital part of the cultural body and could breed only defensiveness. In human service organizations we would do well to be as circumspect as the anthropologist. To do so does not necessarily take intellectual agility or academic training, but it certainly takes sensitivity, respect, diligence, and genuine contact.

7. While it seems a patent truth that an anthropological respect for the culture of minority clientele must guide practice, we cannot ignore the truth that most of the clientele who find their way to human service organizations have spent much if not all of their lives bombarded by the dominant culture. Their cultures are often a confusing mixture of the dominant culture and their own. They have lived with continuing cultural conflict. Some of that conflict has been subtle and the erosion of elements of their culture insidious and covert. Too, some of the instances of conflict have been tense, overt, and demanding. To a degree, the contact of these minorities with human service agencies represents another possibility of threat to the integrity of their cultures and patterns of living. Awareness of this risk makes the initial contact between minority client and human service agency particularly tense and frequently unproductive.

8. We would be foolish, of course, to ignore racism — institutional and individual, aversive and benign — and the patterns of discrimination that operate to deny minorities sufficient and appropriate help. We have artificially dichotomized cultural difference and racism for purposes of analysis and explication. However, we are fully aware that the two combine in a nettlesome variety of ways in the real world. An example of their combination, to our view, is the notion of the culture of poverty. The idea suggests that certain aspects that the dominant group supposes about the poor (frequently meaning by that certain ethnic minorities of color), such as inability to delay gratification, illegitimacy, family disorganization, low achievement motivation, and so forth, are produced from the

generational effects of poverty and inextricably a part of the individual identities and group symbolism of the poor. The problem of such an idea is that the qualities of such a culture, as defined by the majority culture, are undesirable and seen as "causes" of continuing poverty; so they require social exorcism. Not an idle armchair theory, such a notion in all of its forms became a part of the explanation of conglomerate miseries of the poor for human service agencies.[11] Genuine elements of certain minority cultures were redefined. Defensive but adaptive strategies designed to cope with discrimination and deprivation were seen as integral parts of culture and all with the threads of racial bias woven throughout. As a caution, then, to the reader, we do not intend the soft pedaling of prejudice and racism as ignorance of their importance. Rather, the focus of the book is on clash that takes place daily between minority and majority because of ethnocentrism.

CULTURE

Like most constructs in social science, there is continuing debate about what exactly in the real world culture refers to. Ignoring such controversy, we want to make plain our view of culture since it is central to the themes of this book.

Human beings, unlike animals, are not built into the world instinctually with patterns of behavior neatly assured. Rather, humans must construct and construe their world symbolically. The world does not come to us as a given. Rather, at some point, we have had to impose meaning upon it, to set some order to chaos, some predictability to the unknown, and to inject some conviction into the neutral.[12] The primary source of meaning, the symbol system out of which we build a livable world, is culture. And every culture is in some ways a fiction and artifice. We should not assume a homology between the phenomenon of culture and the world external to it. "There is reality," says Robert Murphy, "but there are also representations of reality which are very real to those who live with them. The two are not at all the same. But we do share representations of reality and this legitimizes and reinforces one another's interpretation of it."[13] This is culture, and it consists "of stylistic and ideational models for and of behavior, as well as a system for viewing and interpreting the world."[14] And, once again,

"Ongoing life has a structure, but our ideas of it make it palatable and comprehensible. The world and man's objectification of it are discordant, but this is not the product only of particular times and circumstances. It is, rather, a necessary part of the human situation and an existential condition of society."[15]

We have, then, little or no justification for regarding one culture as superior to another, to be rooted in some eternal verities or smiled upon by the Gods. Instead, each culture is an evolved response to the conditions faced by particular human groups over time. An edifice of beliefs, values, signs, language, styles of relating, and technology, culture continually changes and shifts but is, at heart, human beings' way of anchoring themselves in an immense, impersonal, dangerous, and overwhelming universe. The "mysterium tremendum" confronting us all, as individuals or communities, past and present, requires security, continuity, meaning, and tools for confronting reality. Culture provides that.[16]

It is no wonder, then, that we each boast about and boost our culture before us. Without it we are naked, vulnerable, and, in Fromm's words, "lost in paradise."[17] We are assured, having grown up with it and taken it in as hungrily as nutriment that our view of the world must be right, "the only way" for "it could not be otherwise." Such a view, however natural it seems, is, in Sartre's words "bad faith" — acting as if something were compulsory, which is in fact voluntary. We *could* take any number of views of family, of God, of state, and so forth, but we don't. The symbolic artifice of our culture is too central to our comfort, existentially, as beings.[18]

The personality of each of us emanates from three interacting forces: our feelings about ourselves and the sense of worth we have about our place in our particular cosmology of people, ideologies, and institutions; the actual objects in our transactional field (primarily people, but also things); and, finally, the values and meanings that we attach to the world and ourselves. "These values take the form of rules for navigating in a particular social world, the *rules* are embodied in the *behavior* that we learn deriving satisfaction from this world. . . .we know that man [sic] needs self-esteem and that *it is the primary function of each culture to provide for the continuing possibility of self-esteem for a symbolic animal*"[19] (our emphasis).

The problem we face as human beings, then, is to develop perceptual and cognitive command over a complex world in a way that permits us a sense of self-value, belongingness and rootedness, meaning, and a way to get into the world of objects reliably and securely.[20] Our language, tools, ideologies, and customs — the esthetics of everyday life — do, under the best of circumstances, just that. In a sense, we are an *epiphenomenon of culture*.[21] That is, we don't take culture by choice, rather it is the vehicle of our symbolic birth and life. Such a course would be smooth except that there is always a degree of tension between the cultural image of the world and how we perceive it as individuals; the unity between person and culture is never complete. Cultures are too large; they also embody conflicts and paradoxes and are, in some ways, incomprehensible.[22]

Because elements of culture seep persistently into the bed of our personality and because our sense of the real depends on culture, the attacks on or threats to it are equally threats to our individual identity, integrity, and security and require defending. It is difficult for us to perceive or, if we do see, to accept the viability of another's culture. It is inconceivable to us, down to the marrow at times, that the world might be legitimately otherwise than our construction of it. The popular pejoration, ethnocentrism, is rooted firmly in the circumstance of our being. Thus, encounters between members of different cultural groups, from tourism to diplomacy and from intimacy to formal role performances, have enormous potential for conflict and hostility and most certainly misunderstanding. Intercultural relationships do not always end, of course, in antagonistic eruptions, but the possibility is always imminent. The unfortunate effects of ethnocentric myopia lie strewn everywhere before us. Unfortunately, too, the same may be said of many of the efforts of human service agencies to serve members of different cultural groups. Misinterpretation of their needs, problems, strengths, and resources has cast many helping efforts on the rocks of mutual frustration and resentment. In every organizational structure, we find cultural phenomena embodied, usually of the dominant culture, and the excursions of ethnic minorities to seek assistance in helping organizations are often tentative forays into a strange and uncompromising land.

Culture influences a variety of human activities. To qualify as a genuine cultural system, says Edward Hall, patterned activity, for example childbearing and work, must be rooted in biological requisites, be capable of being analyzed in its own terms, and yet reflect other cultural systems. The cultural systems that Hall outlines include interaction, association, subsistence, bisexuality (gender), territoriality, temporality, learning, play, defense, and exploitation. Each of these is mediated by symbols (language, writing, and nonverbal language) and each has overt and covert aspects. In addition, all systems have formal, informal, and technological forms. As an example, learning (its content and modes) is a system of all cultures. It is rooted in biological givens (all creatures must *learn* in varying degrees to adapt); it is involved with other cultural systems, for example relationships, time, and space; and it has explicit elements, for example the legal and normative requirements of public schooling, and implicit ones (attitudes toward learning and feelings about achievement and success, for instance). Formal learning is that, in school and out, which is taught by precept and admonition. Informal learning might include the modeling of an agent of socialization or learning, and although there are rules that apply to modeling, only when they are broken do they become explicated. Technical learning involves the logical delineation of steps to acquire specific kinds of knowledge and skill, for example becoming a social worker.[23]

The basic coin of all these systems is symbolization and language. Benjamin Whorf has made the most powerful statement of this fact: ". . . the world is presented in a kaleidoscopic flux of impression which has to be organized by our minds — and this means largely by linguistic systems in our minds. We cut nature up, organize it into concepts, and ascribe significances as we do, largely because we are parties to an agreement to organize it in this way — an agreement that holds throughout our speech community and is codified in the patterns of our language. The agreement is, of course an implicit and unstated one, *but its terms are absolutely obligatory.*"[24]

The world of human activity then is pared into many systems and is organized through language, and all systems are imperfectly related to each other. Culture is at heart communication and symbolization, the purpose of which is to provide meaning and order. It is not one thing but many things and the slant on the world that it yields is felt by its members to be valid. "A belief in witches or bacteria as an event or process is to be explained in sociocultural terms rather than neurologic [or psychological — authors] concepts. The *believing* is the response of a human organism to cultural stimulus. But *what* the organism believes is determined not by itself but by its culture."[25]

A subculture, according to Milton Yinger, is a culture that has derived over time some of its elements from a cultural system different than the dominant culture under which it exists. That is, in some of its aspects it is congruent with the dominant culture; in others, there is a kind of imperfect fusion of elements of both cultures, and there are, finally, elements of culture unique to the minority system. Most of the cultures we will discuss in this book would be, by this stricter definition, subcultures.[26]

An Example of the Influence of Culture: Helping/Mental Health

In our society we appear to approve and appreciate the scientific definition and treatment of mental illness (though some critics assure us that our science in this area is metaphorical).[27] In a culture where symbols often suggest technology, science, and a linear world view (the assumption of cause and effect) and where many relationships are assumed to be "professional" the idea that science and technology and their disciples, the professions, can cure ills of all kinds is of a piece. From the selling of underarm deodorants to brake linings and from the designing of a nuclear holocaust to the perfect marriage, science reigns supreme in our culture. Thus, to have a healer (a doctor of medicine, let's say) who is detached in his personal approach to us and extends that distance through the employment of various esoterica and tools is not disturbing to us, but desired. The language of our exchange with the doctor will be based on an association characterized by dominance-submission, the vernacular formal and stilted, and the elements of faith and transcendent belief downplayed, if not entirely forgotten. Such a pattern would extend, for the most part, to our treatment of mental illness as well.

Efforts to bring this cultural medicine show to other cultures or subcultures have often failed. Frequently folk beliefs, tied to the supernatural and magical, have upset the best and most aseptic ministrations of the health or mental health team. The neatness and precision of the clinic only frightens or puts off members of some other cultures and is sometimes no match for the arcane legerdemain of a folk healer. Our usual response is to denigrate the folk healer as phony, likeable perhaps, but a charlatan nevertheless. However, the fact remains that many ethnic groups believe that mental illness has both natural and unnatural causes. Natural causes (psychiatry, for example, tends to zero in on these) might include the effects of malnutrition, generations of poverty and discrimination, genetic deficit, and the mental erosion of drug abuse. Unnatural causes, on the other hand, and equally important, suggest the influence of malign magic, spirit possession, or the malevolent influence of others.[28] Thus, one might find him/herself as the victim of cruel fate (organic psychosis of some kind) *or* the target of the evil ministrations of an enemy. Whatever the cause, the cure must relate to it, and in the latter instance our conceptions and technologies of mental health do not jibe with the cultures'. Among some Hispanics the set of beliefs about unnatural causes is called *curanderismo*; among Puerto Ricans an equivalent belief system called *espiritismo* exists. In both cases there are folk healers who will tend to the illnesses that fall under those rubrics. Among certain subcultural groups of Anglos, beliefs in faith healing, spirit possession, and intermediaries with the spirit world abound. For members of the dominant culture, there are views of unnatural causes that invite the soothing balm of Tarot cards, palm readers, astrologists, and assorted and celebrated gurus.

The point is that attempts on the part of a mental health agency to subvert or demean this other system, even ignore it, can only create more distance and friction between minority clientele and the agency. The two cultures can be complementary and need not be antagonistic. An instructive example is the East Los Angeles mental health agency which, in its initial sortie into this predominantly Mexican-American community, came with Freudian banners flying. Little success followed. Finally when the agency recognized the importance of the parallel health system and the legitimacy and importance of *curanderos,* their place in the community solidified and their work began to produce benefits.[29] There is currently debate on the extensiveness of curanderismo among Hispanic groups. At this point, it is clear that it does exist, but the number of people that rely upon it is subject to question.

So culture affects how individuals define and experience disease, what they expect of helpers, how they perceive the healing relationship, and what technologies and rituals are acceptable to them. Ignorance of this elemental part of life can only bring the ludicrous and sad attempts to cross-cultural barriers that have typified much of human service to this point.

Organizations

Most human services are meted out in an organizational context. As we suggested earlier, the organization itself is a cultural statement and captures elements of culture in its structure, functions, ideologies, and processes. For example we tend to think of organizations as rationalized structures, relatively impermeable and enduring, for providing goods and services. The bureaucratic phenomenon, in its ideal form, proceeds from a scientific-technological ideal, and the root metaphor that guides our thinking about it tends to be a pyramid or a latticework of boxes. The physical structure of many agencies reflects this thinking as it takes on the appearance of various sized boxes beside or stacked on top of each other. As a result, for many organizations alternative modes of being and doing are unimagined or rarely tried, such as the development of indigent resource networks as one level of organizational functioning; outreach programs; cooperative, flexibly defined task forces of clients and staff; provision for consultation; or ombudsmen activities to community groups.[30] One could think of an organization, or at least a part of it, not necessarily as a pyramid but, rather as a pseudopod that can become larger or smaller and can absorb or extrude cultural elements.

Organizations have spawned any number of problems confounding well-meaning attempts to improve the range and pertinence of services to minorities. Bureaucratic jargon, excesses of paperwork, technical complexity, burdensome rules and regulations, and the impersonality of functionaries have all worked to stymie reaching out to potential but culturally different recipients. In addition, the dramaturgy of giving help — the demeanor and manner of helpers, the decor and arrangement of organizational fronts, appearances and impressions given off, and the rituals of helping — often work to create intercultural tension. Seated behind a desk, dressed in a suit, asking personal questions in order to fill out a form, and using stilted language, the helper becomes an imposing and frightening figure. None of this is necessarily so, but the point is that the structure and process of service and the interpersonal esthetics of help must be sensitive to cultural differences.

THE TRANSCULTURAL PERSPECTIVE

The perspective we intend to offer is admittedly rudimentary and meant to provide only guidelines for improving the organizational context in which minority clientele are served. The specifics of the perspective will be fleshed out in each chapter as we discuss particular areas of service.

Two cautionary notes must precede the laying out of the perspective. While we have hammered on the importance of cultural difference, we are aware of the universals of human experience, whether it is child-rearing, mating patterns, a belief in the transcendent, political and social differentiation, the division of labor, play, or anything that we regard as important human activities.[31] No culture is entirely alien to any other, and we would regret any perspective that would paint any culture as a curiosity. We simply are anxious to correct what we judge as indifference and ignorance when it comes to the treatment of other cultures and subcultures in human service agencies.

No doubt, several organizational activities and commitments must precede the successful application of our perspective. Not the least of these is the hiring of staff who are members of minority cultures served by the agency. A second would be to ensure bicultural and bilingual (or trilingual, etc.) education and training for agency personnel. Certainly a commitment at the higher realms of the agency hierarchy to lubricate and tune the relationship between the agency and relevant cultures is essential.

The Cultural System

The starting point of understanding is to begin to grasp and appreciate major elements of the culture as a whole. Since symbols are the key, learning the language is of enormous help. However, even if one does not take that step, becoming acquainted with some of the major values and belief systems is of the moment. Although language and culture are inextricably intertwined, and one cannot expect to *fully* learn the culture without learning the language, it is possible to develop a simple, functional understanding of the world view of another culture. Some of the major preoccupations, the signal constructs of their world, ideas about good and evil, the place of the individual, family, and group in the world of people and nature are part of the cultural system.[32] They are manifest in the habits, rituals, routines, and prosaic transactions of everyday life, from the words between parents and children through ideas about diet to the dynamisms of play and work. A keen observer willing to sensitively engage members of another culture can begin to sense some of the priorities, concerns, and prominent issues in a given culture. To do so requires sedulous commitment and openness but is quite possible.

The cultural system can be divided into four basic systems:

1. *Social relationships and association.*

Clearly we are social animals. It is our prolonged dependency as children and the supremacy of learning over instinct as an adaptive tool that make it so. We are provided with, thanks to culture and social structure, norms, expectations, and roles that guide our meanderings in a variety of social contexts and set our conduct with different categories of people. Such rules and frames solidify and make manageable and somewhat predictable the complexity of relationships with different essences and sensibilities. Many questions must be asked on our way to understanding different cultures.

How do members of the culture perceive friendship, family roles, and responsibilities? How do they view outsiders? What are recognizable categories (roles) of relationships between people? What are the persistent obligations between individuals in different roles? How do individuals perceive the exchanges (giving and taking) in relationships or the obligations of various kinds of association? What are the rules that govern civility and day-to-day contact with others? What are the distinctions between public and private behaviors? What specializations and divisions of responsibilities and labors exist in various social contexts (family, marriage, work, and male and female relationships)? When are relationships seen as problematic? What ideals govern relationships in certain situations and contexts? Answers to these questions help the interested agency and help-giver begin to tap the dimensions of relationships and associations that form the social bonds of the cultural or subcultural community.

2. *The world view.*

We dangle in a cosmology of people, things, natural forces, and mysteries. The potential chaos and the enormousness of our world is toned down through philosophies, values, perspectives, and paradigms. We set a secure foot in this morass thanks to our world view. The discovery of a dominant view for a culture presupposes answers to certain questions.

What are the dominant and orienting values — contemplative, active, ascetic, hedonistic, passive? Is nature seen as something to be conquered or accepted (a frightening, malevolent force or a malleable and bountiful field)? Is the world rational or irrational in its daily machinations and turnings? What is the cultural view of material things? Are they to be acquired or hoarded? Are they markers of success and achievement or are they incidentals in the path of life? Is change and progress prized or regarded as a threat?

3. *The world of action.*

The hardest thing that we must do as human beings is act. To move comfortably with some conviction and continuity in this world is a neat trick. Culture helps us accomplish action as well as orientation. To discover the framework and spur to action, some of the following questions must be answered.

How are people to be motivated (by external or internal forces)? Do people value being or doing? What is the character of the balance between work and play, and how is each defined? How are decisions and choices made and is the context of action individual or group-oriented, egalitarian or authoritarian, or rational or mystical? What are the dominant orientations to others (affiliative, competitive, distant, close, accepting, or circumspect)? How do people mark their lives in terms of time and accomplishment? What are the ways in which people learn and what is the content of learning?

4. *The individual and the world.*

The individual recapitulates, unknowingly perhaps, the struggles of the culture to define a peoples' place. To grow as an individual requires not only the incorporation of cultural meanings and social requisites but their transformation into some sort of unique expression, an identity. Typically, every culture imperfectly and tensely joins with each of its individuals, but in every culture there is a distinctive flavor to each individual. To know this we would ask, at least, the following questions:

What are the primary sources of identity, and how important is the individual in relationship to the group or the larger social con-

text? What is the relative balance between the demands of in-
dividualism and the requisites of the group? How much freedom
does the individual have to define and redefine the self? What are the
typical stages of self-formation?[33]

Innumerable questions in each of these areas suggest themselves.
Much like the ethnographer, the helping agent, under the auspice of
the human service agency, immerses him or herself in the culture
with an attitude of respect, interest, and sensitivity to the importance of the cultural answers to the questions that concern each
human community. The learning of any culture, even one's own, is
always incomplete; it is too big; much of it lies buried beneath the
psychological and social surface, and change is always altering its
facade. Nevertheless, the attempt is absolutely essential.

The social structure: The meanings, values, styles of being, and the
symbolizations of culture manifest themselves through the institutionalized patterns and arrangements of social life. One meets
culture in the day-to-day rituals and habits of life, the network of
roles, statuses, institutional imperatives, and social divisions. In
essence, the structure of kinship and family, economic patterns,
political systems, educational processes, religious institutions, and
aesthetic pursuits are the heart of the social structure. One must
know these to fairly assess and reasonably act within a given culture
or subculture. While it may be, in the dominant culture, acceptable
to sequester one's elder relatives in a nursing home, in a given subculture it may be a basic violation of the remains of the extended
family structure. To invoke oneself as a leader of people over a particular political issue in the dominant culture is acceptable; in
another, one can only emerge as a leader at the request of others. To
make as much money as one can in the dominant culture may be one
of the tests and fleeting ideals of life; elsewhere to make more than
one needs, to accumulate excess for oneself, may border on the
perverse. In the midst of a cardiovascular crisis, for a member of the
dominant culture to submit to the technical intervention of a
defibrillator may seem not only essential but a basic right. In
another community it may be viewed as an unwarranted attempt to
subvert nature's work. The social structure, then, will influence,
perhaps dominate, how people from another cultural group approach a given human service, as it patterns activity on the basis of
essential values and symbols.

The specific concerns of human service agencies: Whether it be a family agency, a child care agency, a health care organization, or an economic policy or program, culture penetrates how people see their problems, what they define as help and the goal of help, and how they adapt to the problem. According to Leininger, some of the following will affect the human service agency as it goes about its work:

1. *The relevant cultural life-style.*

In a family agency, for example, patterns of socializing children, the division of parental responsibilities, the value placed on children, patterns of dominance and submission, and the like become important to know. Any intervention methodology that obviously violates the family life-style is doomed to failure.

2. *Pertinent cultural values and norms.*

Any context and pattern of activities is governed by values, which are difficult to observe, and norms, which are not difficult to observe. In the agency's approach to its problem area, these must be recognized and honored. If it is against familial norms for children to talk back to a parent, to encourage adolescents in a pattern of assertive behavior that smacks of rebelliousness can only confound the problem, not ease it. To suggest a family form of therapy for a cultural grouping that proscribes intimate and personal discussions between parents and children is likewise doomed to failure. Thus, again, keen apprehension of norms and values is requisite for culturally sensitive practice.

3. *Cultural taboos and myths.*

Every culture proscribes a range of behavior through the operation of formal and informal taboos. Every culture also has a panoply of myth by which it explains parts of the world and averts threats to security and existence. Nutritional education in a health agency if uninformed about the dietary taboos and the health-giving myths of certain foods or practices of clientele will certainly fail to a degree in its well-meaning mission to improve the health of a certain population. Members of some subcultures, for instance, refuse to come to the hospital for needed care and attention, not because of fear pertaining to illness but because the nutritional delights of the hospital kitchen suggest violation of some of the food taboos of the would-be patient.

4. *Life caring rituals and rites of passage.*

Every culture has institutionalized and informal rites by which it marks significant life events. Every culture has also developed ritualized methodologies by which it confers health, wisdom, and comfort on individuals. The human service agency cannot defile these rites. They are, to the individual, of more importance than the technological and professional rituals provided by the agency. A well-known rite of passage in all cultures surrounds death. For the dominant culture, the professional orientation to death is primarily one of distance, objectivity, and the scientific conquest of death. Hospitals are well-known for their elaborate organizational denials of the reality of death. To likewise deny the family of a dying patient from another culture the opportunity to invoke the rituals of continuity and passage may create more problems than the death of the family member.

In some other cultures the passage from childhood to adulthood may not have the same meaning or the same ritual paraphernalia surrounding it as in the dominant culture. For the majority culture moving out of the house and becoming independent are the benchmarks of adult status, and a family agency might well work with a family to encourage this important psychological "break." However, some other peoples may see the sign of adulthood as the ability to assume care of the family, to step into the parent's shoes, and to accept the mantle of responsibility from the parents.

Finally, rites associated with caring (or helping) must be honored. Frequently such rites in the informal structure of a culture are quite different than the rites of the helping professional and agency. The discrepancies must be noted and provided for.

5. *The folk healer and the healing system.*

Every culture has folk beliefs about health, happiness, emotional vitality, family integrity, and so forth. Typically, as we have mentioned before, professional orientations to helping denigrate or ignore the folk system. Yet it is a fact that folk systems have survived because they are seen as effective, accessible, culturally relevant, supportive, and embedded in the interpersonal network of the community. Working with such a system rather than denying its existence or effectiveness would seem to be the only viable strategy for the human service organization. That does not mean that the agency must abandon its clientele to the folk system but rather create and tailor its care to complement such a system.[34]

Table 1-I

Contrasting Assumptions of a Transcultural Perspective
on Helping and Helping Organizations with a Monocultural View

Transcultural	Monocultural
1. All cultures are valid and viable.	1. The dominant culture is valid and viable.
2. The organization and methodologies of helping are value-laden.	2. The organization and methodologies of helping are value-free.
3. All aspects of the helping process are infused with cultural symbols, knowledge, and culturally patterned activity.	3. The technologies of helping are culturally neutral and valid in all cultures.
4. The greatest threat to helping ethnic minorities of color is ethnocentrism.	4. The greatest threat to helping ethnic minorities of color is lack of technical knowledge.
5. Cultural sensitivity, awareness, experiential recognition, and affirmation of the cultural factor must precede competent helping of ethnic minorities of color.	5. Cultural sensitivity and knowledge is not central to the helping process.
6. The assessment of and intervention into individual and collective problems is essentially ecological (acknowledging the interdependence of culture, social structure, family patterns, individual difference, etc.).	6. The assessment and intervention into individual and collective problems is essentially individual/adaptive (regarding the individual as the locus of the problem — "Blaming the Victim").
7. Cultural diversity and heterogeneity must be built into organizational structure and process.	7. Cultural homogeneity is taken for granted: organizationally prescribed roles are the basis for behavior.
8. It is the human service organization's responsibility to adjust its structure and function to accommodate cultural difference.	8. It is the responsibility of the culturally different to accommodate to the human service organization.
9. Organizational models should be organic, flexible, and dynamic.	9. Organizational models are linear, rigid, and static.

SUMMARY

It has been our basic view that minority clientele are frequently not served well or at all by human service agencies because the reality of their culture is denied or undermined by those agencies. Culture is ineluctably tied to individual and group identity and cannot be ignored. It is our intent then to demonstrate how human service agencies can employ culturalogical knowledge to embolden and straighten out the relationship they have with minority clientele. We must emphasize, however, some confusions and complications in the matter before we proceed:

1. No culture is unitary. All cultures are riddled with variations and conflicts. Those variations may relate to class, region, or urban-rural location or have no visible tie to any structural or geographical entity.

2. As we have said, minority cultures of our concern are subcultures. That is, they are antic conglomerations of the dominant culture and their own heritage. In spite of that, we believe that our basic perspective still applies, although it may not always seem resonant or unencumbered as an analytic and intervention tool.

3. The influence of culture as opposed to socioeconomic status is not terribly clear. Poverty and deprivation do encourage adaptive life-styles. To assume that they are cultural would be mistaken, we think. Nevertheless, these adaptive patterns, too, must be given credence and be understood. It may be that a middle-class member of a given subcultural group is quite different from a lower-class member, perhaps, in some ways, more similar to a middle-class member of the dominant culture.

4. Racism and its destructive handiwork cannot be underestimated. Though it is not of central concern here, we do give the devil his due. On the other hand, it is our judgment that much racism is founded on cultural conflict and the profound misinformation one culture has about another. It is hoped the development of cultural awareness and learning will render human service agencies less prone to what on the surface appear to be depredations of institutional racism.

REFERENCES

1. Kadushin, Alfred: *Child Welfare Services,* 3rd ed. New York, Macmillan, 1980, pp. 62-67.
2. Solomon, Barbara Bryant: *Black Empowerment: Social Work in Oppressed Communities.* New York, Columbia University Press, 1976, pp. 11-36.

3. Rossi, Alice: Sex equality: The beginnings of ideology. *The Humanist, XXIX*: 3-6, 16, 1969.
4. White, Leslie: *The Science of Culture.* New York, Grove Press, 1949, pp. 143-147.
5. Montagu, Ashley: *Man's Most Dangerous Myth: The Fallacy of Race.* London, Oxford University Press, 1974, pp. 83-86.
6. Murray, Albert: *The Omni-Americans: New Perspectives on Black Experience and American Culture.* New York, Outerbridge and Dienstfrey, 1970, pp. 39-40.
7. Geertz, Clifford: *The Interpretation of Culture: Selected Essays.* New York, Basic Books, 1973, pp. 15-17.
8. Friere, Paulo: *Education for Critical Consciousness.* New York, Seabury Press, 1973, pp. 41-58.
9. Hall, Edward T., and Whyte, William Foote: Intercultural communication: A guide for men of action. *Human Organization, 19*:5-12, 1960.
10. Foster, George M.: *Applied Anthropology.* Boston, Little, Brown, 1969, pp. 6-9; Gans, Herbert J.: *People and Plans: Essays on Urban Problems and Solutions.* New York, Basic Books, 1968, pp. 208-220.
11. Moynihan, Daniel P. (Ed.): *On Understanding Poverty.* New York, Basic Books, 1969.
12. Becker, Ernest: *Escape from Evil.* New York, Free Press, 1975, pp. 128-145.
13. Murphy, Robert F.: *The Dialectics of Social Life: Alarms and Excursions into Anthropological Theory.* New York, Basic Books, 1971, pp. 90-91.
14. *Ibid.,* p.50.
15. *Ibid.,* p.115.
16. Becker, *Escape. . .op. cit.,* pp. 123-127.
17. Fromm, Erich: *The Anatomy of Human Destructiveness.* New York, Holt, Rinehart, and Winston, 1973, pp. 225.
18. Berger, Peter L., and Luckmann, Thomas: *The Social Construction of Reality: A Treatise on the Sociology of Knowledge.* New York, Doubleday/Anchor, 1967, pp. 53-67; see also *Berger's Invitation to Sociology: A Humanist Perspective.* New York, Doubleday/Anchor, 1963.
19. Becker, Ernest: *The Structure of Evil.* New York, George Braziller, 1968, p. 157.
20. *Ibid.,* pp. 174-176.
21. Murphy, *op. cit.,* p. 133.
22. White, *op. cit.,* pp. 336-345.
23. Hall, Edward T.: *The Silent Language.* New York, Doubleday, 1959, Chapters 3 and 4.
24. Whorf, Benjamin: Science and linguistics. *The Technology Review, 42*:231, 1940.
25. White, *op. cit.,* p. 173.
26. Yinger, J. Milton: Contraculture and subculture. *American Sociological Review, 25*:625-635, 1960.
27. Torrey, E. Fuller: *The Mind Game: Witchdoctors and Psychiatrists.* New York, Bantam Books, 1972, pp. 1-12; Szasz, Thomas: *The Myth of Psychotherapy.* New York, Doubleday/Anchor, 1978, pp. 3-10.
28. Winthrob, Ronald M.: Belief and behavior: Cultural factors in the recognition and treatment of mental illness. In Foulks, Edward F. et al. (Eds.): *Current*

Perspectives in Cultural Psychiatry. New York, Spectrum, 1977, pp. 103-111.

29. Karno, Marvin, and Morales, Armando A.: A community mental health service for Mexican-Americans in a metropolis. *Comprehensive Psychiatry,* *12*:116-121, 1971.

30. Solomon, *op. cit.,* pp. 355-381. See also Chapter 9 for an excellent essay on organizational insensitivity to minority (Blacks) culture.

31. DeVos, George A.: The interrelationship of social and psychological structures in transcultural psychiatry. In Lebrow, William P. (Ed.): *Culture-Bound Syndromes, Ethnopsychiatry, and Alternate Therapies.* An East-West Center book. Honolulu, University of Hawaii Press, 1976, pp. 284-297.

32. Kroeber, Alfred L., and Kluckhohn, Clyde: *Culture: A Critical Review of Concepts.* New York, Vintage Books, 1952, p. 357.

33. Leininger, Madeline: *Transcultural Nursing: Concepts, Theories, and Practices.* New York, Wiley, 1978, Chapters 1 to 5.

34. *Ibid.,* pp. 89-100.

Chapter 2

THE TRANSCULTURAL PERSPECTIVE AND
INCOME MAINTENANCE SERVICES

ACCORDING to Spindler the term *public welfare* "lacks a precise definition, a universal acceptance of what it includes, what it covers, what public programs and activities are, how they function, and how effective they are."[1] Since the term is an elusive concept, has several nuances, and is not recognized as a uniform concept, it means different things to different people. To some, for example, public welfare is the garbage heap for human wreckage (the idle, the shiftless, the unemployable, the sick and decrepit, the transient, loafers, malingerers, beggars, and certain ne'er-do-wells).[2] To others public welfare is public financial and social support for the blind, the disabled, the sick, widows, and dependent children.[3] To others, public welfare is "an aggregation of quite distinct programs, grouped together by most states and localities for administrative convenience in a public welfare department but quite independent from each other in purpose, origin, criteria of performance, and logic of development. Still others by contrast, see public welfare evolving toward organic unity of function and purpose, a single whole in which the parts, however specialized in their function, derive their vitality and character from the parent body."[4]

For our purposes, public welfare has reference to a limited set of public (that is tax-supported programs, activities, and agencies of government constitutionally and legally authorized at federal, state, and local levels) and governmental services to individuals and families designed to help them meet financial and social needs. These include income maintenance (also named assistance payments, public assistance, income security, and security welfare payments); health maintenance and food programs for the aged, the blind, the disabled, and the near poor; financial and medical assistance to families for support of dependent children; medical assistance to the indigent and categorically related poor; and housing and social services to eligible individuals and families.

26

Discussion in this chapter focuses on provisions under aid to families with dependent children; aid to the aged, the blind, and the disabled; food assistance; medical assistance to indigents; housing assistance; social services; and aid to individuals and families not eligible for federal assistance.

Somewhat similar to the concept of public welfare, *culture* is a term with multiple if not ambiguous meanings. It is extremely difficult to define in precise terminology because of the many uses of the term. To one person, for example, it may refer to the fact "that human groups are distinguishable by the manner in which they guide and structure behavior and the meaning ascribed; cultures differ in their world view, in their perspectives on the rhythms and patterns of life, and in their concept of the essential nature of the human condition."[5] These perspectives manifest themselves in symbolic and direct ways via socialization processes, language, material artifacts, art, etc. To another person, it may be viewed as the total way of life that orients thinking about the universe and the proper nature of human-to-human and human-to-God relationships.[6] To another, it may refer to those phenomena that account for patterns of behaving that cannot be fully explained by psychobiological concepts.[7]

To avoid further conceptual confusion, we are not going to attempt another definition of culture here. On this matter we refer our readers back to the definition given in the introductory chapter.

The objectives of this chapter are to provide a general orientation to the field of public welfare and income maintenance and to illustrate the interrelatedness of practice in public welfare settings and cultural phenomena. The focus of the discussion will be on public welfare organizations as institutionalized structures for providing income maintenance services and how culture influences the overall operations of these structures. We expect that when the nature of the subject matter is clearer, readers will be able to recognize the importance of culture and how this phenomenon influences public welfare professionals and workers, their practices, and the effectiveness and responsiveness of their helping.

A RESPONSE TO POVERTY: THE PUBLIC WELFARE SYSTEM

Official estimates of the poverty population are computed from the Current Population Survey (CPS) conducted by the U.S. Bureau of the Census. A household is counted as poor when its annual income falls below a predefined standard that was originally based upon a United States Department of Agriculture diet designed to meet minimum nutritional needs.[8] This standard or poverty index represents the federal government's estimate of the amount of money required to meet a family's minimum needs. It varies by family size and is updated annually to reflect changes in the Consumer Price Index.[9] Table 2-I shows the poverty standards for various family sizes for 1977. As one can see from Table 2-I, for a nonfarm (urban) family of four the poverty standard was $6,191 per year. The standards for farm families of varying sizes are 15 percent lower than those for nonfarm families. Similarly, the computed standards for female-headed families are lower than the standards for families headed by males. Commenting on this difference Levy notes, "this difference occurs because all thresholds are based on U.S. Department of Agriculture Emergency Diets in which the cost of a minimally adequate diet for a woman is calculated to be slightly less than the cost of the same diet for a man."[10]

Table 2-I

Weighted Poverty Standards for 1977

Size of Family	Poverty Standard for Nonfarm Family with Male Head
Single person under 65	$ 3,152
Single person over 65	2,906
2 persons, head under 65	4,072
2 persons, head over 65	3,666
3 persons	4,833
4 persons	6,191
5 persons	7,320
6 persons	8,261
7 persons	10,216

From U.S. Bureau of the Census, Current Population Reports, Series P-60, *Money Income and Poverty Status of Families Living in the United States: 1977*. Courtesy of U.S. Government Printing Office, Washington, D.C.

The official Bureau of the Census definition of poverty includes only cash income. Thus it excludes any in-kind incomes from noncash assistance programs such as food stamps, Medicaid, public housing, etc. Expanding the definition to include noncash assistance (in-kind income), however, would introduce a number of formidable problems. For example, in considering a service like Medicaid, is it fair to say that a person with $3,000 income who also received a $2,000 Medicaid operation is as well off as a person with $5,000 income? How does one measure the well-being of a family that was covered by Medicaid but was well throughout the year and thus received no services at all? Issues like these make the measure of in-kind income difficult. The problem is further complicated because few empirical studies have attempted to measure both a household's cash income and the value of noncash benefits it received from public assistance programs.[11]

The following diagram (Table 2-II) presents data on the relative size of the U.S. poverty population using the Census definition of poverty, which includes cash income only. The data indicates that the number of poor people declined absolutely from 39.5 million to 24.7 million and that the poor as a relative proportion of the population declined from 22.1 percent to approximately 12 percent during the time period indicated. Additionally, the number of poor persons has remained relatively stable during the period 1969 through 1977, and the poor as a percentage of the population declined slightly during that period.

Disaggregating data on the total poverty figures by household for three years, 1960, 1970, and 1976, Levy indicates that between 1960 and 1970 the Census count of the poor declined by about 14 million persons.[12] The major portion of this figure represents households headed by able-bodied, working-age males who were in the best position to take advantage of the expanding employment opportunities of the 1960s.

During the 1970s, an era of economic stagnation and rising inflation, aggregate poverty counts remained fairly stable. Over this period the number of poor persons in families headed by aged or disabled individuals declined significantly but the number of poor persons in female-headed households rose sharply. Between 1970 and 1976 for example, the number of female-headed families with children, both poor and nonpoor, increased by 1.8 million, while the number of such families in poverty increased by over ½ million.[13] In 1976 approximately 33 percent of all female-headed households lived in poverty, compared with approximately 7 percent of the households headed by males. Poor families headed by females are less likely therefore to escape poverty than are poor families headed by males. As a result, the increasing number of poor families headed by females suggests an increase in long-term economic dependency.[14]

Table 2-II

Poverty Population According to Census Bureau
Definition of Poverty, 1959-1977

Year	Number of Persons Living in Poverty (in millions)	Percentage of U.S. Population Living In Poverty
1959	39.5	22.1%
1960	40.0	22.2%
1961	39.6	21.9%
1962	38.6	21.0%
1963	36.4	19.5%
1964	36.1	19.0%
1965	33.2	17.3%
1966	28.5	14.7%
1967	27.0	14.2%
1968	25.4	12.8%
1969	24.1	12.1%
1970	25.4	12.6%
1971	25.6	12.5%
1972	24.5	11.9%
1973	23.0	11.1%
1974	23.4	11.2%
1975	25.9	12.3%
1976	25.0	11.8%
1977	24.7	11.6%

From U.S. Bureau of the Census, Current Population Reports, Series P-60, *Money Income and Poverty Status of Families Living in the United States: 1977.* Courtesy of U.S. Government Printing Office, Washington, D.C. Also found in Frank Levy (Ed.), *The Logic of Welfare Reform,* 1980. pp. 9-11. Courtesy of The Urban Institute Press, Washington, D.C.

As noted earlier, the official definition of poverty and official estimates of the number of people who are poor have been criticized because they are based on a family's cash income and fail therefore to take into account the in-kind benefits a family may have received.

Table 2-III

Persons with Incomes in Cash and Food Benefits
Falling Below the Poverty Line, 1976

Characteristics of Individual's Household Head	Number of Persons in Poverty	Distribution of Weeks Worked by Household Heads, 1976			
		0	1-26	27-46	47 or More
Over 64	3.0 million	71%	3%	1%	25%
Under 64, head critically disabled	.9 million	52%	—	—	48%
Neither aged nor critically disabled					
White female	3.5 million	59%	24%	5%	12%
Nonwhite female	3.1 million	62%	18%	5%	14%
White male	5.5 million	22%	33%	13%	32%
Nonwhite male	1.7 million	20%	24%	18%	37%
Total	17.7 million				
Overall Percentage White:		67%			
Overall Percentage Children under 18:		34%			
Distribution by Census Region:		South	44%		
		North Central	21%		
		Northeast	18%		
		West	17%		

From Frank Levy (Ed.), *The Logic of Welfare Reform,* 1980, p. 15, Table 4. Courtesy of The Urban Institute Press, Washington, D.C.

Among the various in-kind benefits, both Medicaid and food stamps are widely received by those in poverty. The conversion of Medicaid and food stamp benefits into income equivalents will drastically alter the official Census poverty count. Table 2-III presents a recount of the 1976 poverty population when the definition of income is expanded to include both cash income and cash equivalent of food stamps and other nutrition programs.[15] The reanalysis of the poverty population contained in Table 2-III indicates that under an expanded definition of poverty the number of persons in poverty drops from approximately 25 million to approximately 18 million, or about 8 percent of the total population. In addition to this revised poverty census, Table 2-III also includes data pertaining to the work efforts of the poor, their residence or geographical region, and their racial and sex characteristics.

The data clearly contradicts the prevailing stereotypes of the poor. The mass media tends to portray the typical poor person as a black female with a number of dependent children, who lives in an urban metropolis and whose husband has deserted her. The picture presented by the data contained in Table 2-III suggests however that this portrait is inaccurate. A more accurate picture would suggest that the poor (1) are white, (2) are concentrated in the southern regions of the country, (3) are children under eighteen years of age, (4) live in households headed by an able-bodied, working-age man, (5) consist of about 20 percent who live in households headed by a person who is over sixty-five years of age or critically disabled, and (6) consist of about 33 percent who live in a household headed by an able-bodied, working-age woman.[16]

Moreover, the data suggest that many of the poor who are able to work do so. Among the able-bodied, working-age white and nonwhite males who headed households, almost half worked for twenty-six weeks or more, while approximately a third work year round. Similarly, among the able-bodied, working-age white and nonwhite women who headed households, over 33 percent worked some time during the year.

GROWTH OF THE PUBLIC WELFARE SYSTEM: A HISTORICAL ANALYSIS

The development of a meaningful system for providing assistance to the nation's poor has been a long-standing problem that has received only sporadic public attention.[17] Historically, the period between 1932 and the start of World War II has generally been viewed as the turning point in the American welfare system.[18] During this period the responsibility for the development of a systematic approach to the provision of public welfare assistance was placed firmly in the hands of the federal government. As a result, the 1930s saw the greatest volume of congressional public welfare legislation in the history of the United States.[19] The single most important piece of welfare legislation developed during this period was the Social Security Act of 1935. This Act established the principle that public welfare was a matter or right for those specified groups who were unemployed through no fault of their own.[20] Moreover, the Social Security Act explicitly recognized that some major causes of poverty in our society were unemployment, injury and disability to workers, and old age.

The recognition and emphasis in this landmark legislation on social and structural conditions as major causes of poverty, rather than individual enterprise or conditions, was a drastic departure from the past.[21] The enabling legislation, as Grønbjerg and his associates note, "distinguished two primary kinds of support: social insurance, where the individual receiving support had contributed to this support, and public assistance, under which the individual had made no direct contribution because he/she was considered physically incapable of doing so because of circumstances beyond his/her control."[22]

Since its inception, the Social Security Act has grown in scope and in the importance of those social programs it specifically authorizes, the public social policies it expresses, and the influence it plays in national and economic affairs. It has been the legislative and statutory mechanism most relied upon during the intervening years from 1935 to the present in order to respond to identifiable social crises and to the problems associated with poverty, unemployment, and economic catastrophies.[23]

The characteristics of the public welfare system need to be clearly identified if a reliable assessment of its function and performance are to be made. Since the 1930s changes in the magnitude of its operations and expenditures are readily apparent to most observers. Horejsi and others, for example, noted that in the 1950s public assistance payments were made to 5,578,000 persons. By the early 1970s, however, the number of persons receiving such payments had risen to approximately 13.5 million. The total expenditures for public social welfare programs in 1950 were estimated to amount to 23.5 billion. By 1970, however, these expenditures had risen to a startling $146 billion.[24] These figures represent increases of almost two-and-a-half times the number of recipients and over six times the amount of dollars spent during a twenty-year period. Similarly, the

Government Accounting Office (GOA) in a recent report indicates that federal income security spending has grown by nearly 250 percent over the past ten years and, as a result, has become the largest part of the federal budget, e.g. the thirty-seven officially labeled income security programs in the 1979 Federal budget cost about $215 billion, which represented approximately 43 percent of the $500 billion budget package.[25] Additionally, state and locally financed programs supplement federal programs or provide assistance to those not categorically eligible for federal aid. Along with the private sector and other nongovernmental charitable expenditures, these programs account for billions of dollars in additional expenditures.

The growth in the number of program recipients and in total expenditures has produced major changes in the way the system operates. Commenting on the ramifications of this growth on the operation of the system, Horejsi et al. state —

> Increased costs associated with larger caseloads have made public welfare too expensive for smaller units of government. Many programs, such as the adult categories, have been shifted to federal control. Ironically, this same problem has caused some programs to be handed back to the States (e.g., Title XX) or to local governments (e.g., Community Action Program Grants-In-Aid). Each of these shifts means reorganization, and each has required budgetary control — both for planning and for administrative control of personnel and programs. Such growth has brought with it new functions of planned communication, centralized administration, and fiscal accountability.[26]

The public welfare system, it can be said, virtually guarantees to all that some of their basic needs (food, clothing, shelter, etc.) will be provided for. Individually public welfare programs serve what are considered to be worthwhile and necessary goals, and collectively they have helped to prevent and eliminate income poverty for millions of Americans. Yet there is still widespread dissatisfaction with the operational components of the system.[27] Numerous critics of the systems have indicated that the program components are too complex and lack significant integration, are too complex and profuse, are administratively inefficient, and are seemingly unmanageable and inadequate in distributing benefits to target populations. In addition to these programmatic shortcomings, there remain unmet needs among eligible program participants, gross inequities in payment and benefit levels, and strong work disincentive effects, and more importantly, there are serious concerns being raised about the nation's willingness and ability to continually meet public welfare needs and stay within politically acceptable spending levels.[29]

By the mid 1970s, the federal government had established over forty income tested welfare programs where prospective recipients had to demonstrate low income to receive benefits.[30] Many of these programs were designed to provide to those who qualified cash assistance, housing assistance, medical care, legal aid, jobs, social services, etc. They were to be administered by a variety of organizations at various levels of government, and together they made up what has been called the "U.S. Welfare System."[31]

Table 2-IV

Major Income-Tested Programs

	Federal, State and Local Cost in FY 1978	Estimated Number of Beneficiary Units During FY 1978
Aid to Families with Dependent Children	$11.4 billion	3.5 million households
Work incentive program	0.4 billion	2.5 million households
Housing assistance (including public housing assistance and rent subsidies)	3.0 billion	4.2 million persons
Food stamps	5.546 billion federal = 0.285 billion state/local	16.043 million
Child nutrition (including school lunch assistance)	2.5 billion	26.0 million households
Supplemental security income	7.1 billion	4.2 million households
Medicaid	18.9 billion (of which $10.7 billion is state/local)	22.8 million persons
Comprehensive Employment and Training Act, Titles II and IV (includes public service employment)	5.0 billion	0.06 million persons
General assistance	1.0 billion	0.6 million persons

From Frank Levy (Ed.), *The Logic of Welfare Reform,* 1980, p.21, Table 6. Courtesy of The Urban Institute Press, Washington, D.C.

Table 2-IV contains a partial list of the most significant means-tested public welfare programs. A brief description of these programs is given in the following sections.

Aid to Families with Dependent Children

Aid to Families with Dependent Children (AFDC) is the successor to the Aid to Dependent Children (ADC) program as established under the Social Security Act of 1935. It has become the largest, most costly, and perhaps the most controversial component of the public welfare system.[32] AFDC's objective, as defined in the Social Security Act, is "to enable each state to furnish financial assistance, rehabilitation, and other services in order to encourage the care of dependent children in their homes, or in the homes of relatives with whom they are living, to help such parents and relatives to attain or retain the capacity for self-support, and to help maintain and strengthen family life."[33] Thus, the purpose of AFDC is to aid "children deprived of parental support or care by reason of death, continued absence from the home, or physical or mental incapacity of a parent."[34] Consequently, eligibility to participate in the program is based on more than financial need alone. Program benefits are made to certain types of families, such as those that include a dependent child who has been deprived of the support and care of his/her natural parent(s).

The Social Security Act established general operating guidelines and specified the federal-state cost sharing arrangements for the program, but left most other matters, including the determination of benefit levels and many aspects of eligibility determination, up to the discretion of individual states. State administration of the program continued, creating what has been described as fifty-four sub-welfare systems each with its own separate set of rules and regulations.[35] Moreover, since many of the basic program boundaries are left to the purview of the states, there are enormous variations in key program elements such that the system is best described as a non-system. For example benefit levels vary for similar family sizes from $101 per month in Mississippi, $148 in Alabama, $188 in Arkansas, $458 in Wisconsin, $450 in Oregon, $476 in New York, and so on.[36]

Each of the public welfare jurisdictions (including the fifty states, District of Columbia, Guam, Puerto Rico, and the Virgin Islands) participating in the federal program has the sole responsibility for establishing a basic needs standard, which may or may not be the same as the official poverty threshold. An applicant's income is compared to the needs standard to determine eligibility. If the applicant's income is below the established standard, the family is eligible for program benefits providing it meets at least one of the other nonfinancial eligibility criteria such as death, continued absence from the home of a parent(s), physical or mental incapacity of a parent(s), etc.

In many states the AFDC needs standard is extremely complex as Barth et al. note in the following comment: "In some states, the need standard is exceedingly complex for it takes into account the individual needs of each family at a level of detail that is staggering. Does the family have to travel to do its laundry? If so, a mileage allowance may be included in the grant. Does the family have life insurance? If so, the basic monthly rate may be added to the grant. The result is a system that rests on the subjective decisions of case workers and, as a consequence, is subject to many questionable variations and errors."[37]

Once an applicant establishes eligibility, the basic benefit is determined. If the family has no income, the basic grant equals all or some fraction of the state's established need standard. While the law requires each jurisdiction to have a needs standard, it does not require that it actually pay that level of benefits. If the family receives unearned income, that is, benefits from the Old Age Survivors Disability and Health Insurance Program, child support payments, alimony payments, etc., it is applied dollar for dollar against the established needs standards in most cases. If the family head is employed, $30 plus one-third of monthly earnings plus an allowance for work-related expenses, such as day-care, transportation costs, etc., are retained by the recipient. The basic benefit level is then calculated taking into account the $30 disregard and the allowance for work-related expenses. The remainder of the head's earned net income (all states reimburse mandatory payroll deductions: income taxes, payroll taxes, and union dues) is applied dollar for dollar against the state's needs standard.

Twenty-six states and the District of Columbia have elected to complement AFDC with AFDC-UP (UP stands for unemployed parent), a similar program open to two-parent families who meet the following conditions: The father has been unemployed (working less than 100 hours per month) for at least thirty consecutive days, has not (without good cause) refused a bonafide offer of employment or training, has six or more quarters of work in any thirteen calendar-quarter period ending within one year of the application for benefits, is registered with the state's employment service, and is not eligible to receive unemployment compensation or insurance.[38]

Since the inception of the AFDC-UP program in 1961, a relatively small number of two-parent families have been included. Boland, for example, estimated that in February 1973 only 5 percent of the nations's total AFDC population was enrolled in the unemployed parent(s) component of the program.[39] Similarly, Spindler states that during December 1975 a total of 120,000 families with 527,000 recipients of which 307,000 were eligible children, participated in the program.[40] Thus it appears that payments to two-parent households is the exception rather than the rule, even in those states currently participating in the program.

Both the AFDC and AFDC-UP programs have work requirements for employable program participants. Such persons must register with the state's official employment service agency for work or training or face the possibility that their benefits may be denied or terminated. At the present time, employable persons receiving AFDC benefits are required to register for training and employment under the Work Incentive Program (WIN), a program designed to deliver job registration, training, and placement services to program participants. The work requirement in actuality is a requirement to register for work or training and to accept a reasonable position if one is available. If there are no jobs or training slots available, however, a nonworking employable participant would continue to receive program benefits.

The aspect of the Aid to Families with Dependent Children program that has raised the most concern among policymakers has been the rapid growth in the number of program participants. In 1960, the program paid benefits to 3 million people per month or about one out of every sixty people in the population. By 1965, the number of beneficiaries had risen to 4.4 million, and by 1971 these figures had more than doubled, with the total number of beneficiaries exceeding 10 million. In December 1975, there were 3.9 million families with 8.1 million children and a total of 11.4 million beneficiaries receiving assistance under the program.[41] One explanation as to why this rapid growth occurred is given by Levy, who states the following:

> The principal cause was a change in behavior among female household heads. As late as 1967, one-third of those eligible to receive AFDC — predominantly low income female-headed households — had not applied for benefits. Some of these households did not know of the program's existence, while others knew about the program but did not want to bear the stigma associated with accepting public aid. In the late 1960's, information about welfare became widely available, and at the same time people became more willing to accept public assistance. By 1972, almost all female-headed households who were eligible for AFDC benefits were receiving them.[42]

Thus, according to Levy, the rapid expansion of the program during the 1960s indicated a willingness on the part of many female-headed households to regard AFDC as a source of ongoing financial support rather than as a source of assistance to be obtained in emergency situations. Moreover, it seems reasonable to suggest that if a female head of household cannot find a job that provides more income than the AFDC program, the chances are she will apply for the program and continue on it as long as her situation remains unchanged.

A widely held misconception about the AFDC program is that it supports numerous able-bodied men, particularly minority men who are viewed as shiftless and lazy. If such men were to receive income assistance at all, it would have to be, in most instances, under the restrictive AFDC-UP program, which, as noted earlier, has an extremely low participation rate (of the 3.5 million families who received AFDC in 1978, only three percent were headed by able-bodied men and were on the AFDC-UP rolls). The composition of the AFDC population in 1975 is presented in Table 2-V. The data clearly point out that seven out of every ten (70 percent) persons participating in the program were eligible children. Approximately three out of every ten (30 percent) recipients were mothers. Of these women, one-quarter were working while another one-quarter were in training, looking for work, or were disabled. The remaining 50 percent of the eligible women were able-bodied, but not working nor looking for work. Fathers comprised less than three AFDC recipients in 100 (3 percent), and of these, half were physically or mentally disabled. In addition, almost 50 percent of all program participants were white.

Supplemental Security Income

The Supplemental Security Income program (SSI), which went into effect January 1, 1974, attempted to consolidate and replace the earlier categorical programs which had provided assistance to the aged, blind, and disabled. The program represented a major departure in public welfare policy in that the federal government assumed primary responsibility for providing financial assistance to the target populations without any state cost sharing provisions, and the federal government is also the chief conduit for administering the program.

Table 2-V

Composition of AFDC Recipients, May 1975

Position in Family	Number (in millions)	Distribution by Current Work Status					
		Employed Full-Time	Employed Part-Time	Actively Seeking Work or Training	Disabled	Other	Total
Mother	3.1	19%	7%	15%	7%	52%	100%
Father	0.3	8%	4%	27%	47%	14%	100%
Children under 18	7.8	–	–	–	–	–	–
Total	11.2						

From Frank Levy (Ed.), *The Logic of Welfare Reform*, 1980, p. 29, Table 8. Courtesy of The Urban Institute Press, Washington, D.C.

The key provisions of the program are (1) a nationally uniform cash benefit level; (2) a 50 percent benefit reduction rate, for example the dollar reduction in cash benefits that occurs when a program participant's earned income increased by a dollar; (3) nationally uniform eligibility requirements; (4) incentives for state supplementation of the basic benefit level, for example the cash benefit received when the program participant has no countable income; (5) federal administration of the basic benefit grant together with incentives for federal administration of state supplements; and (6) fiscal relief for the states in the form of reduced expenditures for public welfare purposes.[43] Currently, the program provides a basic monthly cash benefit of $189 for an individual and $284 for a couple. This benefit can be supplemented by additional payments by the state and, in fact, nearly half of all program participants receive some state supplementation.

The SSI program approaches a national federally administered public assistance program. In all states, the U.S. Department of Health and Human Services pays for and administers the basic federal SSI benefit. States that wish to supplement the basic benefit can either request that D/HSS administer the state supplement or administer the supplement themselves. The Social Security Administration of D/HSS through its more than 1,200 local offices is responsible for administering the overall program, the mandatory supplements of 32 states, and the optional supplements of seventeen of these. State and local public assistance agencies are responsible for administering the state supplementary payments in the 16 states that have elected separate administration. All states except Arizona and Texas are providing mandatory supplementary payments.[44]

The SSI program interacts with other income-tested programs. For example, the dependents of SSI recipients cannot be covered under SSI, but may be covered by AFDC. Disabled children under eighteen years of age, some of whom are in AFDC families, are now eligible for SSI benefits (they were eligible under the old categorical Aid to the Disabled program). Thus some families will benefit from both SSI and AFDC.[45]

In fiscal year 1978, the SSI program distributed cash benefits to 4.2 million households (approximately 5.1 million aged, blind, and disabled persons) at a total cost of $7.1 billion.[46]

Food Stamps

Food stamps are coupons that can be used in place of money in order to purchase domestically produced food items. The goal of the program is to improve the diets of low-income households and to expand the market for domestically produced food. The program is funded and administered by the U.S. Department of Agriculture. Open-ended federal appropriations fully support program benefits while administrative and operating costs are shared with the states.

In 1970, 4.3 million persons received food stamps at a cost of $550 million; in 1973, 13.2 million persons received stamps at a cost of $2.2 billion; in 1975, 17.1 million persons received stamps at a cost of $4.4 billion; and in 1978, approximately 16 million persons participated in the program at a cost of $5.8 billion.[47] Some of the increase in the number of participants resulted from the transfer of individuals from the surplus commodities program to the stamp program. However, the major part of this increase resulted from the rapid rise in unemployment and the simultaneous worldwide inflation of food prices that occurred in 1973-1974.[48] Through the 1973-1974 period, high unemployment among the population caused personal income to lag, and inflation caused food prices to rapidly increase. The interrelationship between lagging personal incomes and rapid inflation resulted in a sharp growth in the number of persons eligible for program benefits by the year 1978.

From the inception of the program through 1978, those who participated in the program had to purchase the food coupons they needed up to a maximum monthly limit. The monthly limit was based on an estimated adequate diet adjusted for family size. In 1978, for example, the limit was $170 per month in coupons for a family of four. The actual price paid for the coupons was based on a family's countable income, that is total cash income minus deductions for rent, utility costs, unusual medical expenses, etc. A family's food stamp benefit or bonus value is derived by subtracting the purchase price of the stamps from the face value of the stamps. The bonus value received by a family is based on family size and countable income and, as a result, families of the same size but with different countable incomes receive different bonuses. Moreover, a rise in the income of a family results in a proportionate reduction in the food stamp bonus. While there is a slight variation between families, for most of them the costs of purchasing food stamps increases $2 for each $10 increase in the family income.

The criteria established to determine eligibility for participation in the program differed from those of other income-tested assistance programs in several important ways. First, the program is the only one with an income test that is open to all of the poor. It is open to single persons, families with and without children, male-headed families, and female-headed families providing their countable income falls within the established maximums. Second, its income maximums or limits are relatively liberal. In 1977 for example, a family of four could participate in the program as long as its countable income was less than $6,084. Because of the liberal income limits many families whose income exceeded the eligibility limits for most State AFDC programs were able to participate in the program. Third, the program is one of the few means-tested programs in which program beneficiaries have to purchase benefits. As beneficial as the food stamp program has been to the poor and near poor, it has not been without its critics. Some of those critical of the program have objected to the fact that some program participants have had very high gross incomes and are still able to participate in it. Other critics have objected to the purchase price requirement, maintaining that it fosters administrative inefficiencies and places unwarranted burdens on those with very low incomes. In response to these criticisms, Congress acted in 1977 to modify several features of the program. Effective in 1979, therefore, the purchase requirement was eliminated, income eligibility limits were lowered, and allowable deductions were tightened.[49] As a result, the current program is focused on meeting the food needs of individuals and families with relatively low incomes.

Medicaid

Medicaid or medical assistance is the program designed to enable states, at their option, to furnish medical assistance to public assistance beneficiaries and the medically indigent or those individuals and families that do not receive money payments from public welfare programs and whose income minus medical expenditures are less than 133 1/3 percent of the states' established needs standard.[50]

The program was initiated in 1965 as Title 19 of the Social Security Act and is administered entirely by the states. The federal government shares the costs of the program with the states, and it has given the states considerable discretionary powers in determining which medical and related services will be covered.[51]

Each state Medicaid program (all states have a medical assistance program except Arizona and Alaska) must provide coverage for public assistance recipients as long as they are eligible to receive monetary benefits from the programs. As soon as a recipient's income exceeds the welfare break-even level or the level of earnings at which a program's recipient would be ineligible for benefits, Medicaid status changes from full benefits to partial or no benefits. In those states that do not have a separate program for the medically indigent, recipients who become ineligible to participate in the program because of an increase in earnings retain Medicaid eligibility for up to four months.[52]

States that have elected to participate in the Medicaid program are required to reimburse physicians, hospitals, nursing homes, and other medical vendors for all services included on a specified list of minimum services.[53] In addition, states may choose to expand this list of services but do not have the option of contracting it, if they are to receive federal reimbursement. Since states have considerable flexibility in establishing income eligibility limits (the maximum income permitted to qualify for the program is generally 133 percent of a state's AFDC income limit) and benefit coverage and since the cost and availability of medical services vary from state to state, there are wide variations among states in benefit payment levels and participation rates.[54]

Since the inception of the Medicaid program, it has been marked by a rapid increase in the number of participants and escalating costs. In 1967, for example, total expenditures from all levels of government amounted to $2.3 billion. By 1978, however, expenditures for the program had risen to $18.9 billion of which $8.2 billion was paid by state and local units of government. Similarly, in 1975 more than 9 million persons received health care under the program. By 1978, more than 22 million persons participated in the program.[55] The rapid growth in both the number of program participants and in total program expenditures appears to have originated for three reasons: (1) an increased number of states decided to offer the program during the early 1970s; (2) within the states, an increased number of female-headed households had enrolled in the AFDC program (which meant automatic eligibility for the program); and (3) service costs continued to rise on account of a general inflation in the price of medical services and the rapid expansion of the nursing home industry.[56]

Housing

Another key component in the public welfare system is the various housing programs. At present the low income population is aided through a variety of federal housing programs administered by the U.S. Department of Housing and Urban Development or HUD. Most of HUD's housing programs are income-tested and are oftentimes characterized by eligibility criteria and benefit structures that relate the cost of local housing to the beneficiaries' income. For example, in the rent subsidy program there is a rental charge that is set at 25 percent of income with a maximum at the "market rent" (or at the cost for housing owned by the local government or a nonprofit organization). The difference between the rent charged the tenant and the market rent is the subsidy, which falls to zero when 25 percent of the tenant's income equals the market rent.

In 1973, the combined budget for the various housing programs was $2.0 billion and was tied to about 2.2 million housing units. In 1978, approximately 2 million households at an annual cost of $3 billion received housing subsidies.[57]

Like many other social programs, federally assisted housing programs have come under increasing criticism. First, they tend to be inequitable in the sense that there are substantially fewer subsidized units than there are eligible families, and second, housing assistance programs give the consumer little or no choice among housing alternatives, since the programs provide indirect subsidies that are funneled through the current suppliers of housing services.[58]

Programs for the Provision of In-Kind Services

In addition to the programs described above, there are other income-tested programs that provide benefits primarily in the form of goods and services rather than in cash. Included in this group are the health care programs that provide direct services, child welfare services, social services to individuals and families, legal aid services, manpower training services, and child nutrition programs, including school lunch assistance.

At present, policies governing the provision of social services to individuals and families are contained in the Social Service Amendments of 1974 (P.L. 93-647 approved by Congress January 4th, 1975). This legislation, known as Title 20, took effect October 1975 and placed a $2.5 billion ceiling on federal funds for social services. Available funds were to be allocated to states on the basis of their population with 90 percent of the funds to be used for the provision of services to actual welfare recipients. Moreover, the legislation required that services were to be directed toward the following goals: (1) achieving or maintaining economic self-support to prevent, reduce, or eliminate dependency; (2) achieving or maintaining self-sufficiency, including reduction or prevention of dependency; (3) preventing or remedying neglect, abuse, or exploitation of children and adults unable to protect their own interest or preserving, rehabilitating, or reuniting families; (4) preventing or reducing inappropriate institutional care by providing for community-based care, home-based care, or other forms of less intensive care; and (5) securing referral or admission for institutional care when other forms of care are not appropriate and providing services to individuals in institutions.[59]

Title 20 defined two categories of program beneficiaries: (1) public assistance recipients and (2) other low-income persons with a gross monthly income that does not exceed 115 percent of the state's median income, adjusted by family size. A state must charge a reasonable fee for services to people whose gross income is above 80 percent of the state's median income as adjusted for family size and may charge fees for persons with gross family income that does not exceed 80 percent of the state's median income, adjusted for family size.[60]

Under the auspices of Title 20, individual states have the option of dividing their territory into geographic regions and providing different types or levels of services in the various regions. Services can be provided through a range of different settings, subject only to the limitations of the current federal regulations. For example services can be provided in the home, hospitals, nursing homes, neighborhood community centers, schools, etc. They may be provided by a staff social worker of the state, county, or city welfare department, a social worker of a community agency, a professional in private or group practice, etc. In addition, services may be offered singly or in combination to individuals, families, groups, and communities.[61]

The range of services that can be provided for under Title 20 are extensive and may include such services as problem identification and diagnosis, personal and family counseling, treatment of problems, rehabilitation and follow-up, information and referral, etc. Current federal regulations, however, specify that certain services will not be reimbursable under the law unless they are integral components of other social services.[62]

The Omnibus Budget Reconciliation Act of 1981 calls for amending Title 20 of the Social Security Act in order to establish block grants for the provision of social services. States would be allocated a share of total funding of $2.4 billion in 1982, $2.45 billion in 1983, $2.5 billion in 1984, $2.6 billion in 1985, and $2.7 billion in 1986 and thereafter. The amount of money each state receives will be based on the state's population size according to figures derived from the 1980 Census. Title 20 will therefore continue as an appropriated entitlement, but states will no longer be required to provide matching funds. In addition, each state is authorized to transfer up to 10 percent of its annual allocation between the health, energy assistance, and social service block grants without prior federal approval.

General Assistance

Most states and localities have a cash transfer program variously referred to as general assistance, general relief, home relief, outdoor relief, emergency relief, or direct relief. The major objective of the general assistance (GA) program is to provide emergency or short-term assistance to persons not eligible for other federally assisted cash payment programs to help them meet their basic need for food, clothing, shelter, or special needs not elsewhere obtainable. Federal legislation and federal participation in general assistance programs is absent. Aspects of program operation, such as eligibility determination, coverage, benefits, policies, administrative arrangements and methods, etc., are determined solely by the states. As a result, general assistance programs vary considerably among the states, between counties in many states, and within counties in some states.

In sixteen states, general assistance is limited to short-term or emergency cash or in-kind assistance. Many states in addition provide continuing assistance to families or individuals under certain conditions. For example in some states, continuing assistance may be limited to unemployable individuals or to families with no employable members, or assistance may be provided to a family when the wage earner is unemployed or unemployable. In a few states, earnings of the low-income working poor may be supplemented on a continuing basis with general assistance funds.[63]

Expenditures for the various general assistance programs during 1975 totaled $1.2 billion, of which $1.1 billion was in the form of cash payments to eligible recipients. The remaining amount was used to pay for medical care services of program participants. The number of households participating in the various general assistance programs totaled approximately 667,000 in 1975. This figure represented some 964,000 different recipients. The number of recipients participating in the general assistance program during 1978 dropped to about 600,000 with program expenditures dropping to approximately $1 billion.[64]

DIMENSIONS OF PUBLIC WELFARE ORGANIZATIONS: THEORETICAL APPROACHES

The income maintenance programs described in the previous section are the major components of the current public welfare system. All of them are, to a certain extent, income-tested, which by definition means they provide benefits to those individuals and families whose incomes are below some predefined level. The provisions, benefits, and services offered by these programs are made available to target populations generally through the operations of large-scale formal organizations, that is, the majority of persons involved in providing services are employed in complex organizational settings. As a result, these employees are required to deal with the constraints inherent in the organizational environment that surrounds them, i.e. lines of authority to which they are accountable, rules and regulations within which they operate, and organizational boundaries they must learn to negotiate.[65] As long as such organizations continue to be the major conduit for public welfare services, it is important that we understand some of the characteristics of these organizations and some of the ways these characteristics may influence the delivery of services to target populations. In this section, we will review some of the theoretical traditions that are useful for understanding the structure and dynamics of public welfare organizations.

The first tradition, the classical bureaucratic approach, concerns itself with the formal structure of the organization, that is the rational arrangements that would produce the most efficient social mechanism for organized activities. Among the best known theorist in this tradition is Max Weber. He held the view that the monocratic bureaucracy was the most efficient, precise, and rational means of organization. As he believed the following: "Precision, speed, unambiguity, knowledge of the files, continuity, discretion, unity, strict subordination, reduction of friction, and of material and personal costs — these are raised to the optimum point in the strictly bureaucratic administration. As compared with all collegiate, honorific, and avocational forms of administration, trained bureaucracy is superior on all these points."[66]

Bureaucracy represented for Weber a specific type of legal-rational authority that could be distinguished from organization of individuals bound together through charismatic or traditional authority. His ideal of the bureaucracy was a large scale organization with a high degree of specialization, hierarchical authority structure, impersonal relationships between organizational members, appointment of officials on the basis of merit and technical knowledge, a priori specification of job authority, separation of policy and administrative decisions, and formal rules that govern those relations not specified by the above.[67]

In the post-Weberian development of organizational theory, an organization came to be viewed as an adaptive organic whole rather than solely a rational legal system.[68] Gouldner, in his writings, has called this the natural system model of organizational analysis. From this perspective the organization is conceived as a purposely designed instrument to achieve specific goals and a cooperative enterprise that seeks to survive and maintain its own equilibrium. This quest for survival, according to this model, may continue even after the attainment of organizational goals.

The adaptive organic whole model of organizations was followed closely by another school of thought: the structural-functionalist perspective.[69] Structural functionalism expanded the study of organizations to include such dimensions as external pressures on the organization, the conflict between organizational needs and personal needs, informal and formal relations, and the effects of the environment on the organization.[70] Further, the structural functionalist enlarged the scope of organizational analysis to include such organizations as schools, social welfare agencies, hospitals, prisons, etc., in conjunction with economic and industrial organizations.

The second tradition in the study of large-scale organizations, scientific management, was concerned not with ways in which the organization could serve people but with the various ways in which people could serve the organization.[71] Taylor, the founder of the scientific management school, believed that for every organizational task in industry, there is one best way of performance or way of doing a job that could be scientifically determined.[72] Once these scientific principles were identified, a careful delineation of requirements for each worker's job could be made, thus ensuring effectiveness and maximum productivity as defined by management. Scientific management assumed that if you controlled people, you could likewise control their productivity, that is, the worker was viewed as an instrument of production that could be manipulated as a nonsocial object.[73]

The human relations theorists realized that the problems of productivity and efficiency were far more complex than that suggested by scientific management.[74] They stressed the need for the management of the organization to address itself to issues such as styles of supervision and leadership, worker's sentiments, motivations, morale, and social relations as they affect work performance. The human relations approach was, therefore, social psychological, and as such it emphasized the informal structures found in the organization, for example leadership styles, job satisfaction and morale, problems of intergroup relations, interest groups, feelings and attitudes, and authority.[75]

Similar to the ideas expressed in the scientific management approach, writing in the human relations approach also asserted that there was a "one best way" to organize work relations in order to increase productivity. What was needed, however, was a form or organization that permitted the worker's autonomy, provided for participatory democracy in decision making related to the workers task, and in general, was cognizant of related aspects of the formal dimensions of the organization. Moreover, this approach to organizational analysis developed a set of normative prescriptions designed to resolve the inevitable problems between the individual and organization. In so doing, it attempted to develop an ideal model of organization in which there is a perfect balance between the organization's goals and the worker's needs.[76]

Recent developments in organizational theory have begun to make explicit the political character of organizations, that is organizations are conceptualized as political systems. Thus, emphasis is given to the problem of power and conflict as these social processes relate to the distribution of and control over resources, people, decisions, and policymaking and the development of organizational goals.[77]

This brief overview of organizational theory and analysis has utility for helping us to understand the structure and dynamics of organizations and their environment. However, many of the approaches discussed come under considerable criticism when we attempt to examine them in relation to people processing and people serving organizations, such as public welfare agencies. It has been assumed by many organizational theorists that the constructs and propositions useful in understanding business, industrial, and economic organizations can be helpful in understanding the functioning of human service organizations.[78] Drucker, a noted business management theorist, argues, however, that borrowing from either business or industrial administration, or both, is quite inappropriate for people serving organizations because of important qualitative differences in the characteristics of these organizations.[79] Some of the major differences between human service organizations and industrial organizations are the intangibility of goals and objectives, criteria for determining efficiency, bases for budgetary allocations, indeterminancy in the measurement of both outcomes and outputs, and the criteria for successful performance. In general agreement with Drucker's analysis, Sarri and Hasenfeld further assert that human service organizations are a distinct and unique set of organizations because of the following characteristics: (1) human service organizations work on people by processing and/or changing them individually or collectively (the persons handled by these organizations are simultaneously their input, raw material, and product); (2) human service organizations are characterized by a precarious domain, that is these organizations confront multiple expectations and conflicting demands that are likely to result in the development of ambiguous and often contradictory goals; (3) human service organizations, particularly those in the public sector, acquire very limited autonomy in relation to their task environment (they are highly dependent on resources controlled by other organizations and are often subject to extensive regulations by various legislative and administrative bodies); and (4) despite the increase in the variety of new technologies, a major characteristic of these organizations is the lack of determinate and effective technologies, which, in the long run, results in a great deal of internal organizational ambiguity and inconsistencies in response to clients served by these organizations.[80]

Having discussed some of the salient theories of complex organizations and having identified and discussed the key characteristics of human service organizations, we shall turn our attention to a discussion of the interface between public welfare organizations and cultural variables. In addition, attention will be given to strategies and techniques in the helping process that can be of utility in making these organizations culturally sensitive to the diverse groups they serve.

THE HELPING PROCESS: THE INFLUENCE OF CULTURE

The fact that income maintenance and support services are provided through formal organizations represents an important aspect of the public welfare system. It is the organizational environment that provides a common meeting ground for the providers and the recipients of services. The recipients of services do not enter the organizational setting lacking in cultural values. They bring with them a social and moral identity that cannot be ignored or overlooked by those responsible for providing services. Moreover, recipients are members of diverse reference groups who exert influence on them and their motivational and behavioral responses. They are self-activating persons whose responses are determined, in part, not only by their immediate situations, but also by their desires, motivations, attitudes, and past learning and conditioning. Consequently, when individuals enter the organization in their roles as service recipients, organizational service providers must be sensitive to their backgrounds and cultural traditions in order for the services provided to be meaningful and effective.

Cultural values influence the relationship between the service providers and clients in several ways. First, the cultures of the service providers, who have socialized them to accept certain assumptions and values as true, are significant factors impacting the relationships. Second is the culture of the clients, who likewise have been socialized to accept certain values and assumptions about reality. Third are the assumptions inherent in the problem itself, which may derive from a culture quite different from that of either the provider or recipient. Finally, there is the culture of the organization in which the relationship is occurring, and this environment will impose its own restrictions and opportunities on the relationship.[81] Each participating culture will impose its own demands on what constitutes a satisfactory solution to a given problem. Consequently, service providers need to be aware of the culture-specific aspects in the helping process, in their particular helping styles, and in the organizational settings in which services are provided so that they can deal more skillfully with the cultural variable.

Rapport and Structure

The helping process is a psychological interaction involving two or more individuals. One or more of the actors in the process is considered to be able to help the other person or persons live and function more effectively at the time of the involvement or at some future time.[82] The goal of the helping relationship is to assist, directly or indirectly, the recipient (or recipients) in adjusting to or negotiating the environments that influence his or her well-being. To accomplish this goal, the service provider must relate to and communicate with the recipient, must determine the recipient's state of adjustment, must decide alone or with the recipient the course of action needed to improve the recipient's current or future situation, and should be able to intervene at some level of competency to assist the recipient.[83] Thus, the helping process suggests ipso facto, the establishment of a mutual bond between the various participants. The emotional bridge between the service provider and the recipient is referred to as rapport. Simply defined rapport connotes a comfortable and unconstrained mutual trust and confidence between two or more persons.[84] In the helping process, rapport is the existence of a mutual responsiveness that encourages the participants to react immediately, spontaneously, and sympathetically to the sentiments and attitudes of every other participant. As Vontress notes, "Rapport should not be misconstrued as involving only the initial 'small talk' designed to put the counselee at ease. Rather, it is a dynamic emotional bridge that must be maintained throughout the counseling process. During the relationship, the participants continuously take stock of each other. They notice how the other presents him/herself, what is said and how it is said. The nature of the communications, explicit or implicit, can cause the counselee, or even the counselor, to alternate from trust to tacit reserve or even to overt hostility."[85]

Differences in racial or ethnic background, in culture, in socioeconomic class, and in language oftentimes make it difficult for professionals of the dominant cultural group to establish rapport with individuals from other cultural groups.[86] However, it is possible to identify some general guidelines that can be of help in this regard. First, the professional helpers should try to avoid extremes in behavior. They should refrain from over or underdressing, that is they should dress so as not to unduly call attention to themselves. Second, the professionals should curtail small talk in the beginning of the helping relationship, especially if they don't know what small talk is appropriate. Small talk may be perceived as an attempt by the professionals to delay the unpleasant. As such, it can be anxiety producing for the participants in the helping process. The professional helpers should start the initial interview with a direct, but courteous, "How can I help you?" This will allow the client to chitchat if he/she is uncomfortable going immediately into his/her reason(s) for seeking help.[87] Third, professionals have the responsibility for structuring the helping process. They should, very early in the helping process, structure or define their role to clients, that is they should indicate what, how, and why they intend to do what they will do. It is important to communicate to the client(s) what is expected of everyone involved in the helping process. Failure to structure the process early and adequately can result in unfortunate and unnecessary misunderstanding because the professional's interests and concerns have not been made clear to other participants. Finally, professionals working with minorities need to realize that they may be working with persons who, because of their cultural and ex-periential backgrounds, are unable or unwilling to participate in introspective explorations. Therefore, techniques such as prolonged silences should be avoided, at least until positive rapport has been established, for their use tends to become awkward and to increase the distances between the professionals and their clients.[88]

Resistance, Transference, and Countertransference

Resistance generally refers to the client's opposition to the goals and objectives of the helping process. It may manifest itself in a variety of ways, such as self-devaluation, intellectualization, and overt hostility. For example many young blacks appear to be shy and withdrawn in the helping relationship. The professional unfamiliar with the nuances of black culture may assess the behavior as another unfortunate effect of social and economic deprivation. However, the client's perception of his or her own behavior may be very different; he or she's just cooling it until he/she is convinced that the professional is a person of good will.[89] On the other hand, such clients may be profusely talkative and refuse to let the professional "get a word in edgeways." Although such deportment may be perceived as an indication of positive rapport, it can also mean that the client is "playing along" with the professional, in essence, being resistive to help.

Another example of resistance among minorities in the helping process is failure to show up for an appointment. American Indians and low-income blacks, for example, may agree to come in for an interview or conference, when in fact they have no intention of following through. They promise to do so out of courtesy, respect, or fear.

Transference refers to an individual's reacting to a person in the present in a manner similar to the way he or she has reacted to another person in the past.[90] It may be conscious or unconscious or positive or negative, and it is considered a form of resistance to the goals of the helping relationship.[91] Transference is especially important in the majority-minority helping process because minority group members bring to the relationship intense emotions derived from experiences with and feelings toward the majority group. For example, black children learn at an early age that white people are not to be trusted. As they mature in decaying ghettos of great cities, blacks also have other experiences that lead them to approach whites with resentful anxiety, distrust, hostility, and ambivalence. Thus, in the helping relationship, blacks appear to be fearful, shy, and reluctant to talk.

The counterpart of transference is countertransference. It occurs when professional helpers react to particular clients as they have reacted toward other similar persons in their past. It may lead to persistently inappropriate behavior toward the client and result in untold strains in the helping relationship.[92] Although professionals are quick to recognize transference as a reality, they find it difficult to consider the possibility that they may not accept, respect, or like many of their clients.[93] Their professional training has inculcated in them the tenet that they should behave toward all in an empathetic and congruent manner. Therefore, they fail to admit that they are human beings with a variety of attitudes, beliefs, and values that invariably affect the helping relationship that they have established with minority-group people.

One of the manifestations of countertransference in the helping relationship, is what Vontress describes as the *Great White Father syndrome*.[94] He states the following:

> Because majority-group members occupy the most powerful and prestigious positions in society, they are often perceived, rightly or wrongly, by minority-group people as being authoritarian and condescending. Majority-group counselors may communicate to minority-group clients that they are not only omnipotent but that they mean their clients nothing but good. They literally guarantee them that they will deliver if the client will put themselves in their hands. Simultaneously, they communicate, albeit unconsciously, the implication that if the clients do not depend on them, they will be doomed to catastrophe.[95]

The Great White Father syndrome may be interpreted as countertransference because it suggests that the professional is anxious to demonstrate not only his/her power and authority but also to prove that he/she is not like the other majority-group people the minority client may have known.

Another manifestation of countertransference is the professional's tendency to be excessively sympathetic and indulgent with minority clients. For example, the professional's definition of achievement for minorities may be different than for members of the majority group. If a different set of achievement criteria are considered appropriate for minorities than for the dominant cultural group, the professional is guilty of saying, thinking, or condescendingly implying that the minority-group client is pretty good for a black, a Mexican-American, or an Indian.[96]

Language

Language is a part of an individual's culture. Failure to understand another's language is failure to comprehend much of another's culture. In order to communicate effectively with minority-group clients, the professional must be able to understand the verbal and nonverbal languages of his or her clients.

Professionals encounter varying degrees of difficulty when communicating with racial and ethnic minorities. For example American Indians of whatever tribe communicate with great economy of language, and they are given to the use of concrete words as opposed to abstract ones.[97] Therefore, professionals find that Indian clients are limited in the ability to express personal feelings, which are considered important in the helping process.

In working with black clients, professionals often experience difficulties in understanding the verbal and nonverbal languages used by this group. They oftentimes misunderstand the slangs, idioms, and slurred pronunciations endemic to blacks (in particular lower-income blacks) and, as a result, not wanting to appear ignorant of the client's argot, they become more confused as to what the client is saying, As Vontress states, "If the counselor fails to understand the client for whatever reasons, the most honest thing to do is to ask him for an explanation or repetition of his statement."[98]

Minority-group clients, as we all do, speak not just with their voices; they use their entire bodies either to make statements or to punctuate them. For example Beier has noted that young black males tend to sit in a slouched position with their chin in hand and unconsciously wipe at the chin or mouth with their hand when there is nothing visible to wipe away.[99] These nonverbal expressions are filled with significant meaning to one who can interpret them. To arrive at the correct interpretation of the meanings of gestures, postures, and inflections, the professional must come to understand the group, their institutions, values, and culture.

Knowing the client's language is important because so many traditional interventive approaches and techniques require fluency in this area. An accurate interpretation of what the client is saying presupposes a fundamental working knowledge of the client's everyday language. In order to know what the client is experiencing or feeling, the professional must be able to accurately understand the verbal and nonverbal behaviors of his or her clients. The professional must not allow skin color or accent to blind him or her to cues that would or could be important in the relationship with minority group clients.[100]

Psychosocial Barriers in the Helping Process

One of the most important psychosocial characteristics of racial and ethnic minorities that influences the helping process is that of self-disclosure. Self-disclosure can be defined as the willingness to let another person know what you think, feel, or want. Self-disclosure is crucial to the rapport-establishment phase of the helping process because it is the means by which clients make themselves known to their professional helpers.

Reluctance to disclose can be a problem in the helping relationship when the helper is white and the one needing help is a minority-group member. For example blacks are especially reluctant to disclose themselves to others because few blacks perceive whites as being individuals of good will who can be trusted. They will only disclose themselves when they feel they can trust the professionals, who in most instances are white, not necessarily when they feel that they are being understood.[101] In fact, black clients often fear being understood because it carries with it the idea of loss of autonomy, being known, and being engulfed in a society they perceive as racist. It is conceivable that, as Vontress notes, "In the case of the black client, the counselor who understands too much is to be feared or even hated."[102]

When working with Hispanic males, it is important to understand the psychosocial characteristics of machismo. Machismo refers to one's manhood, the manly traits of honor and dignity, to the courage to fight, to keeping one's word, and to protecting one's name.[103] In addition, it refers to a man's running his home, controlling his women, and directing his children. Therefore, machismo is not to be taken for granted. It suggests clear-cut separation of the sexes, that is males enjoy rights and privileges denied women, who are generally reluctant to demand equality.[104] Moreover, machismo as a cultural value expresses itself as a general inability or unwillingness of Hispanic males to verbalize or ventilate their feelings. Expressions of inner feelings are seen as signs of weakness. To openly discuss or communicate such feelings, even within the context of the family, is socially discouraged.

An important implication of machismo is that majority-group female professionals should not be too aggressive or too forward in the helping relationship when the clients are Hispanic males. If the helping process is to be effective at all, the right amount of deference must be shown at all times. This may be particularly difficult in a context in which we are being sensitized to the inequities of a sexist society.[105]

Another important psychosocial characteristic among racial and ethnic minorities is that of personalism. This concept suggests that individuals are more interested in and motivated by considerations for people than they are for bureaucratic protocol. Professionals who are enslaved by clocks and adhere to appointments, promptness, and protocol are often the object of suspicion by their minority-group clients. In the helping process, personalism requires that the professional get his or her clients to make and keep appointments. Minority-group clients, however, prefer to drop by to visit and may get around to discussing something that has been bothering them while they are there.

Rendering professional help requires, in part, an ability to listen. Many minority-group clients, however, have little experience in this area, probably because of their early socialization experiences. For example, lower-income blacks generally come from large families in which their homes were filled with din and confusion and with everybody talking simultaneously. In such an environment, people learn not to listen to what words mean but to the emotions the speakers convey.[106] This is why the professional may discern a blank stare on the face of his black client. The empty facial expression indicates that the client has tuned out the professional until he/she stops talking. The inability of many black clients to listen may help explain why their conversation seems to have little continuity of ideas.

These, then, are some of the more salient cultural and psychosocial characteristics that may influence the participants in the helping process. They are discussed to illustrate the importance of the need for the professional helper to be aware of culturally specific factors when in interaction with culturally diverse clients.

DELIVERING INCOME MAINTENANCE SERVICES: THE NEED FOR CULTURAL SENSITIVITY

The effective delivery of income maintenance services demands that providers of service be able to relate to and communicate with members of diverse racial and ethnic groups. Not only must they be able to establish rapport with these clients, but they must be able to accurately ascertain the clients levels of need, resources available to clients to resolve identified needs, the levels of social and psychological adjustments of clients, and so on. Providers of service are expected to make realistic recommendations designed to assist their clients, and more importantly, they must be able and willing to intervene personally to assist them.

To accomplish these goals, professionals must become cognizant of themselves. They must be consciously aware of their own values, attitudes, beliefs, prejudices, and behavior toward racial and ethnic clients different from themselves. This suggestion is supported by Pedersen et al., who note the following:

> As the counselor works with persons belonging to a life-style different from his own for any length of time, he participates in and contributes to a process of acculturation by himself and his clients. The counselor may assist his client to choose cultural assimilation, where the dominant culture enforces its adoption, integration, and where its best elements are incorporated; or adaptation, where the individual or group accommodates to the dominant environment; the counselor who is himself undergoing acculturation must first recognize those characteristics of his own style of behavior, attitudes, beliefs, and personal assumptions that will allow him to experience another culture as a means of learning about that culture. Otherwise, the therapist may substitute his own self reference criteria of desired social effectiveness for alternative criteria more appropriate to the client's environment.[107]

Moreover, professionals must recognize that individuals from culturally different groups do vary according to the degree to which they have become acculturated or assimilated into the dominant or mainstream culture. For example some individuals may lose their total cultural identity; some may accept aspects of the dominant culture while simultaneously retaining many components of the old; some may become bicultural, moving comfortably back and forth across the lines separating the old culture from the new; or some may remain essentially immersed in their own culture because they are excluded physically and psychologically from the dominant culture.[108] Thus, the degree to which the individual is assimilated in the dominant culture determines the specific ways in which the individual perceives or conceives of his or her environment and strongly influences his or her values, attitudes, and behavior.

As has been pointed out, professionals are expected to make realistic recommendations designed to help their clients, and they must be able to intervene personally to assist them. Often, however, professionals are unable to intervene effectively on behalf of their clients for several important reasons. Minority-group clients themselves may be resistant to the goals of the helping process. Such goals may involve behavioral and/or attitudinal changes that clients are unwilling to accept. In addition, the acceptance and attainment of helping goals can be blocked by the clients' families and friends, who may not see the relevance of such goals in resolving the presenting problem(s). In such situations, professionals may need to expand the helping process to include family members and significant others in order to provide needed help to the target client(s).

Providing meaningful help to minority-group clients can frequently be made difficult because of the organizational settings in which such help is given. Hispanic clients, for example, have traditionally had trouble entering and negotiating bureaucratic helping systems because their cultures and languages constitute major handicaps. As a result, services delivered to these clients have been ineffective in resolving their many problems. Black clients, too, oftentimes have difficulties in organizational environments because many of the employees in these environments or organizational settings are overtly and covertly hostile to their presence. Services delivered in hostile or racist settings are bound to be ineffective at worst and partially effective at best.

SUMMARY

The cultures represented by the providers of services and cultures of the organizations through which services are delivered can be supportive, neutral, or antagonistic to the cultures of minority-group clients. When these many cultures interface within the context of the helping process, they can ignite cultural conflict on the part of the participants in the interaction. For example cultural differences between service providers and their clients may act as significant barriers to the service delivery process in several ways. First, there are apt to be sets of misfitting expectations. There may be differences in the definitions and evaluations of the client's problems by the service providers and the clients themselves. There are also likely to be different expectations concerning the appropriate role of the professionals in the helping process. If the differences in expectations lead to increases in social distances between service providers and clients, it is likely that there will be important differences in how problems are defined and what strategies are most appropriate for resolving them. Second, cultural differences can lead to differential ordering of problems and priorities by service providers and clients. Because cultural differences imply differential experiences and values, the ways in which the client's personal resources, for example, time, money, energy, etc., are to be used will vary between the workers and clients. That is there may be culturally determined differences in the way service providers and clients feel about the allocation of the client's personal resources to resolve problems. Lastly, cultural differences between service providers and their clients can influence helping relationships negatively because of the differential vulnerabilities to the egos involved in the helping process. For example the helping relationship may be of such a nature that it implies threats of punishment and/or deprivation for the client; it may imply threats of victimization at the hands of a strange and noncaring service provider; it may also imply threats of ridicule or blame for not behaving as the service provider believes people should behave; or it may involve threats of failure in the face of strongly sanctioned behavioral or attitudinal norms.[109] The extent to which cultural differences may be operative in the helping process must be determined by the professional helper. Moreover, every effort must be made to control their negative influence on the nature and structure of the service rendering process.

Those who provide services in public welfare organizations are products of a culture that has been characterized as racist.[110] In their undergraduate, graduate, continuing education, and in-service training, they need to be exposed to new experiences if they are to be effective when working with minority-group clients. Although, as Vontress so aptly notes, "A course in counseling racial and ethnic minorities may be another exciting and rewarding cognitive exposure, what is needed most are affective experiences designed to humanize counselors."[111] Such experiences as living in the cultural environments of the minority groups served by the organization, conducting research endeavors with and on behalf of minority-group communities, having field education placements and internships in minority communities, etc., are a few realistic ways for helping service providers become sensitive and aware of cultural parameters and how these parameters influence their abilities to deliver income maintenance services.

REFERENCES

1. Spindler, Arthur: *Public Welfare.* New York, Human Science Press, 1979, p. 13.
2. Skidmore, Rex A., and Thackeray, Milton, G.: *Introduction to Social Work.* Englewood Cliffs, New Jersey, Prentice-Hall, Inc., 1976, p. 99.
3. Spindler, *op. cit.*
4. Wickenden, Elizabeth, and Bell, Winifred: *Public Welfare.* New York, Columbia University Press, 1961, p. 13.
5. Devore, Wynetta, and Schlesinger, Elfriede G.: *Ethnic Sensitive Social Work Practice.* St. Louis, C.V. Mosby Co., 1981, p. 9.
6. Valentine, Charles A.: *Culture and Poverty: Critique and Counter Proposal.* Chicago, University of Chicago Press, 1968.
7. Kaplan, David, and Manners, Robert A.: *Culture Theory.* Englewood Cliffs, New Jersey, Prentice-Hall, Inc., 1972.
8. Orshansky, Mollie: Counting the poor: Another look at the poverty profile. *Social Security Bulletin, 28*:3-29, 1965.
9. Levy, Frank: *The Logic of Welfare Reform.* Washington, D.C., The Urban Institute, 1980.
10. *Ibid.,* p. 6-8.
11. *Ibid.*
12. *Ibid.*
13. *Ibid.*
14. Ross, Heather L., and Sawhill, Isabel, V.: *Time of Transition: The Growth of Families Headed by Women.* Washington, D.C., The Urban Institute, 1975.
15. Levy, *op. cit.,* p. 11.
16. *Ibid.,* pp. 13-15.
17. Plotnick, Robert D., and Skidmore, Felicity: *Progress Against Poverty: A Review of the 1964-1974 Decade.* New York, Academic Press, 1975.

18. Grønbjerg, Kristen, Street, David, and Suttles, Gerald D.: *Poverty and Social Change.* Chicago, The University of Chicago Press, 1978.
19. Piven, Frances F., and Cloward, Richard A.: *Regulating the Poor: The Functions of Public Welfare.* New York, Pantheon, 1971.
20. Grønbjerg, et. al., *op. cit.,* p. 47.
21. Spindler, Arthur: *Public Welfare.* New York, Human Sciences Press, 1979.
22. Grønbjerg, et al., *op. cit.,* p. 47.
23. Spindler, *op. cit.*
24. Horejsi, John E., Walz, Thomas, and Connolly, Patrick R.: *Working in Welfare: Survival Through Positive Action.* Iowa City, University of Iowa School of Social Work, 1977.
25. *U.S. Income Security System Needs Leadership, Policy, and Effective Management.* United States Government, General Accounting Office Memorandum, Comptroller General's Report to the Congress, Washington, D.C., 1981.
26. Horejsi, et al., *op. cit.,* pp. 40-41.
27. Piven and Cloward, *op. cit.*
28. Barth, Michael, C., Carcagno, George J., and Palmer, John L.: *Toward An Effective Income Support System: Problems, Prospects, and Choices.* Madison, Institute for Research on Poverty, University of Wisconsin-Madison, 1974.
29. *U.S. Income Security System Needs Leadership, Policy, and Effective Management, op. cit.*
30. Spindler, *op. cit.*
31. Levy, *op. cit.*
32. Handler, Joel F., and Hollingsworth, Jane E.: *The Deserving Poor: A Study of Welfare Administration.* Chicago, Markham Publishing Company, 1971.
33. Barth, et. al., *op. cit.*
34. Levy, *op. cit.*
35. Barth, et. al., *op. cit.*
36. Levy, *op. cit.* pp. 23-25.
37. Barth, et. al., *op. cit.,* p. 18.
38. *Ibid.,* p. 16.
39. Boland, Barbara: Participation in the Aid to Families with Dependent Children Program (AFDC). In Joint Economic Committee, Congress of the United States, Subcommittee on Fiscal Policy, *The Family, Poverty, and Welfare Programs: Factors Influencing Family Stability.* Studies in Public Welfare, Paper No. 12 (part 1), Washington, D.C., U.S. Government Printing Office, 1973.
40. Spindler, *op. cit.,* p. 83
41. *Ibid.*
42. Levy, *op. cit.,* p. 26.
43. Barth, et al., *op. cit.,* p. 23.
44. Spindler, *op. cit.*
45. Barth, et al., *op. cit.,* p. 23.
46. Levy, *op. cit.*
47. *Ibid.,* p. 30.
48. *Ibid.,* p. 31.
49. *Ibid.,* pp. 32-34.

50. Barth, et al., *op. cit.*, p. 22.
51. Levy, *op. cit.*, pp. 34-35.
52. Barth, et al., *op. cit.*, p. 22.
53. Levy, *op. cit.*
54. Schultze, Charles L.: *Setting National Priorities: The 1973 Budget.* Washington, D.C., The Brookings Institute, 1973.
55. Levy, *op. cit.*, p. 35.
56. Holahan, John: *Financing Health Care for the Poor: The Medicaid Experience.* Lexington, D.C. Heath and Company, 1975.
57. Levy, *op. cit.*, p. 38-39.
58. Barth, et al., *op. cit.*, pp. 22-24.
59. Spindler, *op. cit.*, pp. 130-148.
60. *Ibid.*, p. 132.
61. *Ibid.*, p. 138.
62. *Ibid.*, pp. 139-142.
63. Barth, et al., *op. cit.*
64. Spindler, *op. cit.*, pp. 119-122.
65. Gilbert, Neil, Miller, Henry, and Specht, Harry: *An Introduction to Social Work Practice.* Englewood Cliffs, New Jersey, Prentice-Hall, Inc., 1980.
66. Gerth, Hans, and Mills, C. Wright (Eds.) and translation from Max Weber: *Essays in Sociology.* New York, Oxford University Press, 1946, p. 214.
67. Hasenfeld, Yeheskel, and English, Richard A.: *Human Service Organizations.* Ann Arbor, The University of Michigan Press, 1974.
68. *Ibid.*, p. 26.
69. *Ibid.*, pp. 25-32.
70. Etzioni, Amitai: *Modern Organizations.* Englewood Cliffs, New Jersey, Prentice-Hall, Inc., 1964.
71. Hasenfeld and English, *op. cit.*, pp. 27-29.
72. *Ibid.*, p. 28.
73. *Ibid.*, p. 29.
74. Whyte, William F.: *Organizational Behavior: Theory and Application.* Homewood, Illinois: Richard D. Irwin, Inc. and the Dorsey Press, 1969.
75. Gilbert, et al., *op. cit.*, pp. 185-188.
76. Hasenfeld and English, *op. cit.*
77. Zald, Mayer N.: *Power in Organizations.* Nashville, Vanderbilt University Press, 1970, pp. 221-261.
78. Sarri, Rosemary C., and Hasenfeld, Yeheskel: *The Management of Human Services.* New York, Columbia University Press, 1978.
79. Drucker, Peter: On Managing the Public Service Institution. *The Public Interest (Fall), 33:*43-60, 1973.
80. Sarri and Hasenfeld, *op. cit.*, pp. 3-5.
81. Pedersen, Paul, Lonner, Walter J., and Draguns, Juris G.: *Counseling Across Cultures.* Honolulu, The University of Hawaii Press, 1976.
82. Vontress, Clemont E.: Racial and ethnic barriers in counseling. In Pedersen, Paul, Lonner, Walter J., and Draguns, Juris G., (Eds.): *Counseling Across Cultures.* Honolulu, The University of Hawaii Press, 1976, pp. 42-64.

83. *Ibid.*, p. 44.
84. *Ibid.*, p. 45.
85. *Ibid.*, p. 46
86. Pedersen, et al., *op. cit.*, pp. 1-16.
87. Vontress, *op. cit.*, p. 47.
88. *Ibid.*, p. 48.
89. *Ibid.*, p. 51.
90. Greenson, Ralph R.: *The Technique and Practice of Psychoanalysis.* New York, International Universities Press, 1964.
91. Vontress, *op. cit.*, p. 51.
92. *Ibid.*, p. 50.
93. *Ibid.*, p. 50.
94. *Ibid.*
95. *Ibid.*
96. *Ibid.*, p. 51.
97. *Ibid.*
98. *Ibid.*, p. 52.
99. Beier, Ernst G.: *The Silent Language of Psychotherapy.* Chicago, Aldine Publishing Company, 1966.
100. Vontress, *op. cit.*, p. 53.
101. Jourard, Sidney M.: *The Transparent Self.* Princeton, D. Van Nostrand Company, 1964.
102. Vontress, *op. cit.*, p. 54.
103. Steiner, Stanley: *La Raza.* New York, Harper and Row Publishers, 1970.
104. Vontress, *op. cit.*, p. 53.
105. *Ibid.*, p. 54.
106. Weller, Jack E.: *Yesterday's People: Life in Contemporary Appalachia.* Lexington, University of Kentucky Press, 1966.
107. Pedersen, *op. cit.*, pp. 22-23.
108. Vontress, *op. cit.*, p. 58.
109. Berkanovic, Emil, and Reeder, Leo G.: Can money buy the appropriate use of services? Some notes on the meaning of utilization data. *Journal of Health and Social Behavior, 15*:93-99, 1974.
110. Pedersen, et al., *op. cit.*, pp. 17-41.
111. Vontress, *op. cit.* p. 62.

Chapter 3

THE TRANSCULTURAL PERSPECTIVE AND
SERVICES TO THE AGED

THIS chapter examines policy issues affecting the delivery of services to aged minorities, services to the minority aged in organizational settings, and some possible avenues of approach in respect to working for change with and on behalf of the minority aged. The first section of the chapter on policy issues affecting the delivery of services to aged minorities examines the overriding conservative mood in American society, and with that, a seeming desire on the part of many to curb welfare state growth. Also discussed is the growth in the number of aged and minority aged, the strain on scarce resources, the particularly vulnerable status of low income minority aged, and race and class factors. The second section of the chapter, which is about services to the minority aged in organizational settings, discusses the complexion of policymaking and organizational staffing with respect to minority aged (and minority) underrepresentation, criticisms of the bureaucratic nature of these organizations regarding the needs of the minority aged, and some of the problems experienced by professionals in bureaucratic organizations that purport to serve the minority aged. The last section of the chapter, which is about working for change in aging services with and on behalf of aged minority consumers, discusses the political context of change efforts and efforts with and on behalf of the minority aged in the political arena and within human service organizations serving the minority aged.

This chapter is not a descriptive overview of all policies, programs, and services to the minority aged. Some important programs such as Social Security are not discussed in any length. The reader is referred to many of the fine publications on the minority aged mentioned in the list of references that do provide a thorough descriptive portrayal of these services. Rather, the emphasis here is more analytical than descriptive, focusing on several key issues that seem important in respect to examining broad transcultural perspectives in human services to the minority aged.

An important point here that has echoed throughout this book is the importance of culture and cultural variables in understanding, planning with and for, and working with the minority aged. Aging itself is "a cultural as well as biological process."[1] Culture, which Herskovits notes is the human-made part of the environment,[2] has impact on the aged in appreciable ways. "Ethnic diversity in the United States persists in the consciousness of individuals, in their perceptions, preferences, behavior," states Michael Novak, "even while mass production and mass communications homogenize our outward appearances."[3] Culture incorporates sets of parameters, acceptable options, possible solutions, and future scenarios. Culture does provide a kind of basic security, and security is something that older people need and earnestly seek. Culture can provide for the aged a sense of time, a sense of place, a sense of continuity and tradition, and a sense of belonging. Ethnicity, ethnic variables, and culture: These are psychological, social, philosophical, and human realities in respect to the minority aged.

Another important point here, which perhaps hardly needs to be stated, is that low-income minority elderly constitute a segment of the population much in need. The needs of the minority aged, considerable as they are now, will grow even more in the future. These needs are growing at the very time that American society appears divided about the future of social services and about the future of the welfare state. Indeed *divided* may be too cautious a word to employ here: There does appear to be a concerted effort on the part of many to curb what has appeared to many to have been an excessive involvement by government in the lives of citizens. This subject of intense political discussion must be our starting point in any rational discussion of services to minority aged.

POLICY ISSUES AFFECTING THE DELIVERY OF SERVICES TO AGED MINORITY CONSUMERS

Policy issues affecting the delivery of services to minority aged consumers are many.[4] Yet these very issues are dwarfed by a much larger issue that drives to the very heart of a social service state. A more conservative mood in American society toward the social services and social welfare did not simply arrive with the election of President Ronald Reagan in 1980. Indeed, the administration of

President Jimmy Carter (1976-1980) was certainly not characterized by a noticeably large (comparatively speaking) commitment to social service spending. In comparison to some Democratic presidents who had preceded him, Carter was much more moderate, even conservative, in political philosophy. The election of President Ronald Reagan has seen a far more deepened and extensive commitment to conservative thinking on the role of government in respect to social welfare. This conservative thinking might be characterized as a minimalist view of the role of government in general (except in respect perhaps to criminal justice and national defense). Philosophical underpinning for this conservative approach can be found in recent works by Robert Nozick,[5] Michael Novak,[6] George Gilder,[7] and others; by black scholars, such as Thomas Sowell;[8] and journals, such as *The Public Interest* and *Commentary*. In short, it is safe to say that a more conservative shift has taken place in America in recent years, both in the electorate and in the intellectual community as well. The marked difference in thinking represented in the 1971 work of John Rawls,[9] (which has often been looked at as a kind of philosophical buttress to liberal social thought) and that of Nozick and others in the mid and late 1970s mentioned above is quite noticeable.

The creation of the Older Americans Act in 1965 and the subsequent amendments to that legislation and other legislation have brought a considerable number of social services to the aged. The aged now compose a significant segment of the social service consumer public currently receiving public benefits, states Robert Hudson, far out of proportion to their numbers.[10] Yet, though services, programs, etc., serving the aged are seemingly numerous and far reaching, it is important to remember that the contrast between the "sweeping objectives of the Older Americans Act and the limited authority provided to the Administration of Aging and other agencies created and supported under the act points to the symbolic nature of the act."[11] One study concluded that after more than a decade of expanded government interest and support, the aged nonetheless find themselves losing ground, with their economic position growing worse year by year.[12] Inflation itself, of course, has wreaked damage on low-income minority aged, as it has as well on other segments of the aged population. What little savings they may have, or what little money they may have, has dwindled in value. The dilemma of an expanding elderly and minority elderly population on the one hand and a conservative, "tough" societal attitude on social welfare and social policies on the other hand is historic and momentous. There appears to be a significant segment of American society that would like to "turn back the clock" on the American welfare state.[13] Many neoconservatives argue that too much is expected of government and of politicians,[14] and government cannot fill all of those expectations. "Running a welfare state is an expensive business," states John Logue, "cheap only in comparison to war."[15] It costs too much, the government can't do the job anyway, and further, government *shouldn't* do the job: The refrain echoes and budget cuts ensue. Unfortunately, the minority aged, susceptible and vulnerable as they already are (even in the most comprehensive "welfare state"), become even more vulnerable.

The minority aged are a growing presence in American society. Black aged (sixty-five and older) numbered 1,556,000 in 1970, 1,989,000 in 1978, and 2,085,826 in 1980. The black aged are projected to be at 3,037,000 by the year 2,000.[16] Official 1980 census data on minority and white aged is indicative of the growing presence of the minority aged in the total aged population. Persons of Spanish origin (sixty-five and older) numbered 708,785 in the year 1980.[17] The Hispanic aged will (like the Hispanic population in general) be growing rapidly in size in the years ahead. American Indian and other minority aged remain quite small in comparison to the black and white aged. Nonwhite aged are expected to grow in number in the decades ahead, "increasing their proportion of the elderly population from about one-tenth to one-sixth in the year 2035."[18] Older blacks and Hispanics are heavily concentrated in urban areas, especially inner cities, and older American Indians as well to an increasing extent.[19] Approximately 5 percent of the older population does not speak English. Of these, 30 percent speak Spanish, 20 percent Italian, and the rest speak a number of other languages.[20]

Census data on the minority aged are not very reliable in the opinion of many. Even the U.S. Census Bureau itself has recognized by its own estimate that the 1970 census misses 2.5 percent of the total population — 5.3 million people or one out of seven Hispanics, one out of fourteen blacks, and one out of fifty whites.[21] The lack of good, reliable census data on the minority aged only compounds problems for policymakers and indeed for everyone alike. "Efforts by, for, and within advocate groups have been hampered by a critical lack of information by which planners, decision-makers, politicians and others can accurately assess the extent and parameters of specific problems. . . . Social policy for the elderly in the United States has generally considered the elderly to be white, English-speaking, and relatively well educated."[22] The Administration on Aging has moved in recent years to change this orientation and has made some progress, but much more needs to be done.

What can be gleaned from the census data on the economic plight of minority aged is not particularly heartening. In 1980, U.S. Bureau of Census estimates derived from the 1980 Census were that of the total elderly population (age sixty-five and older), 13.6 percent of whites were below the poverty level, contrasting sharply with 38.1 percent of blacks and 30.8 percent of Hispanics below the poverty level.[23]

Poverty and low income correspond closely to poor housing, poor health, and other conditions. Among blacks, despite poorer health, there is generally less use of medical services and less frequent visits to physicians by blacks than whites.[24] Minority elderly live in poorer housing. Even the public housing that is available becomes problematic at times because it is sometimes the case that when minority aged eligible for public housing apply, the "less desirable" and often those with the greatest housing needs are rejected.[25]

Social Security is the most widespread program for minority and other aged,[26] and at the same time the program has experienced severe financial problems and has been the subject of much discussion in recent years.[27] Many minorities have either not applied for Social Security, were never enrolled, or were ineligible to enroll. The early Social Security program did not include domestic servants and farm laborers, thus tending to exclude many minorities from the program. Many minorities today, despite the wider overall coverage of the Social Security program, find the program to be confusing and beyond understanding. The bureaucratic forms, complicated procedures, and the rest tend to keep many minorities out of the program, even though they might be eligible for benefits. Some aged minorities have felt that they did not want to reduce their earnings, which are so necessary for their daily existence. The issue of living long enough to be eligible or to receive benefits has already been reiterated and is particularly an issue with males.

Since 1965 with the advent of Medicare and Medicaid, the average number of physician and dentist visits by the minority aged have increased, but such figures can be deceiving in respect to the problems that many minority aged have experienced with these programs. Some of the problems mentioned above in respect to Social Security are similar: excessive paperwork, bureaucratic procedures, lack of comprehensive coverage of the programs, and the like. Many physicians and dentists will not accept Medicaid patients; this is a problem in urban areas and perhaps even more so in many rural areas (where the minority aged person may live many miles away from a physician or dentist agreeable to participating in the program). Some items, eyeglasses, for example, cannot be purchased under Medicare.

Income maintenance, housing, health and mental health, transportation services: the list goes on and on of inadequate, ill-maintained services to low-income minority aged. One would like to paint a brighter picture of human services to the minority aged. Indeed, those minority aged who are in middle- or upper-income brackets (certainly not large in respect to the total) are at more liberty to employ more and better services. But only to a point: Skin color, social class, and aged status accompany the minority aged person wherever they go, and indeed on to the grave itself.

The double jeopardy thesis brings together aged status and skin color under one genus. The National Urban League released a report in 1964[28] that described the double jeopardy of being both old and black in American society. The minority aged suffer the devaluation of old age, parallel in some ways to the devaluation of old age found in most modern societies.[29] But older blacks also suffer the extra hardships of a lifetime of poverty, poor education, and racial discrimination. In this sense they are in double jeopardy.

Since blacks were the first minority people of color to form an organized and coherent civil rights and consciousness raising movement, it was only natural that such a concept would emerge as applied to the black experience. But other minority peoples of color were soon to arise — Hispanics, Indians, and Asian Americans — and the concept of multiple jeopardies has been applied to their experiences as well.[30] Blacks, Hispanics, and other minority elderly living in inner cities suffer increased jeopardy in respect to crime and other urban problems.[31] Certainly the concept of jeopardy could be broadened to include handicaps as well. A handicapped black or Hispanic low-income elderly woman walking through a high crime ghetto area may be more at jeopardy in respect to crime, for example, than a woman of her same description who is not handicapped.

The concept of double or multiple jeopardy has been the subject of some controversy. Ethnic differences in morbidity, mortality, and in many other areas have been discussed in this chapter and throughout the book. The Ten-State Nutrition Survey, which was undertaken between 1968 and 1970, compared the nutritional intake of black, white, and Hispanic elderly (age sixty and older). Gender and income accounted for some of the differences, but in general the study showed that white elderly had a higher nutritional intake than blacks and Hispanics.[32] While these and many other studies point to the poor overall conditions in which low-income minority elderly find themselves in American society, Cantor states that "the cultural patterns of the Black and Hispanic communities, particularly the extended or augmented family structure and value system, tend to mitigate role loss and social isolation."[33] Traditional thinking has held that the minority aged have kinship networks and social support systems at their disposal, while the white aged do not have. This may be particularly true of Hispanics, where self-identity itself has historically been intimately tied to family identification.[34] Murillo has drawn a vivid portrait of the traditional Mexican-American family.[35] However, how much real assistance is provided for the Mexican-American, other Hispanic, and other minority aged by families, kinship networks, social support systems, and the like is difficult to assess. Some minority scholars and others have feared that empirical or other research pointing to the existence of stronger social support systems in minority communities might be used by some to withhold political support for services and programs to minority aged. The history of racism and classism in American society (and in other societies) would appear to underscore some of the fears expressed here.

One recent debate that to some extent has cast a new light on the double-jeopardy or multiple-jeopardy question is that of the renewed interest in the respective roles of race and class in respect to understanding the situation of minorities (and in turn the minority aged) in American society. The black sociologist William Julius Wilson brought this debate into sharper focus with the 1978 publication of his book, *The Declining Significance of Race.*[36] A debate on the pages of *The New York Times Magazine* in 1980 between Kenneth B. Clark and Carl Gershman[37] underscored the dimensions of the discussion. There would appear to be some amount of sentiment building in the minority scholarly community that race and racism may have been stressed too much over class perspectives. The New Left movement of the 1960s or leftist scholarship in general[38] represented by journals such as *The Review of Radical Political Economics* and others has influenced the direction of this debate. The phenomenon of black flight, whereby the black middle class flee the inner city with its lower-class minority populations, is familiar historically among whites, but not as much so among minorities. Hence some have pointed to the gulf between middle- and lower-class minorities and have pointed to the class dimension of capitalist (or socialist) societies (and have not necessarily held Marxist views in so doing).

The double- or triple-jeopardy thesis, if accepted, would now be anchored as well on a specific class dimension. The discussion would appear to focus at times on race subsumed under class rather than the other way around. If the pendulum would appear to swing too far in the direction of class as an explanatory variable, however, then race would appear to be too diminished in import. It is "not an either/or situation; the rising significance of class does not necessarily signal 'the declining significance of race'. . . . In statistical terms, the increment of the social class main effect is accompanied not by a decrement of the racial main effect but by a stronger interaction between class and race for a wide variety of important dependent variables."[39]

Barrera would agree that both class and race are important, co-linked concepts. Barrera favors a left-internal colonial model, which weights class heavily, but race and ethnicity are not forgotten or banished from theoretical view.[40] Milton Gordon's term *ethclass*, which refers to the subculture that is created by the conjoining of ethnicity and class,[41] would appear to be salient here. The concept of ethclass combines both ethnicity and class and by so doing also underscores the importance of both. Social policies and programs serving the minority aged must be designed in such a way that full cognizance is encouraged of the many jeopardies to which the minority aged are subject and of the seminal importance of ethnicity, race, and culture. Beyond all this is the throbbing reality of class as a permeating, fundamental reality.

SERVICES TO THE MINORITY AGED
IN ORGANIZATIONAL SETTINGS

Many social service organizations that deliver social services to minority aged are striving to be as responsive as possible to the many needs of the minority aged. Many senior citizen centers, for example, attempt to do all in their power to provide services that are as attuned to the cultural makeup of the surrounding community as possible, for example providing recreational and other activities of particular interest to particular ethnic and minority aged. But there are problems that abound as well. This section discusses several problem areas in respect to the delivery of services to the minority aged in organizational settings.

It should be stated first that the minority aged, all aged, and indeed any human person, lives in a world of organizations. These organizations have certain mandated goals and are oriented in such a way as to attain or strive to attain these mandated goals. Indeed, Parsons defines formal organizations in terms of their "primacy of orientation toward the attainment of a specific goal."[42] From here we must ask the necessary question of who sets the goals that formal organizations are striving to attain. That leads us to a first concern with policies, for indeed it must be remembered that social service organizations carry out social policies.

Social policy can be defined as "considered strategies for action on problems or needs of a social nature."[43] "Policy" itself is "generally interpreted as meaning an organizing principle to guide action,"[44] or as Kahn states, the "explicit or implicit core of principles, or the continuing line of decisions and constraints, behind specific programs, legislation, administrative practices, or priorities."[45] Most of these strategies for action or organizing principles guiding action are not made by minorities, minority aged, low-income whites, nor women. Most members of the United States Senate are white, middle- and upper-class males. A good percentage are millionaires. Most members of state legislatures are also white, middle- and upper-class males. Indeed, the political scenario is instructive: Much, if not most, social policies on the aged are formulated by a certain segment of the American population.

Legislative bodies can be looked at as organizations of a sort, with organization cultures. "Organization cultures" are "the learned beliefs, values, and characteristic patterns of behavior that exist within an organization."[46] This is not to imply a set uniformity in major legislative bodies, only to state that there are certain patterns that can be noticed and identified; there are certain values, beliefs, and attitudes that a wealthy white Congressperson does not share and cannot share with an elderly black low-income person on a fixed income in a decaying inner-city area. Perhaps stating this is too obvious, but in reiteration it nevertheless should be stated: Legislative bodies that formulate social policies (and other policies) in America are not representative of the heterogeneous mix of the population itself, either according to race, ethnicity, class, or sex.

The human service organizations that carry out aging policies, such as Area Agencies on Aging, Senior Citizen Centers, and Public Welfare Departments, are staffed with a somewhat more heterogeneous mix of people. Even here, whites are predominant, with more white females at lower levels and more white males at the administrative levels. Interestingly, social work, "the reputedly female profession, is led by men. They have planned its policies, determined its academic curriculum, directed its practices, and decided where and for whom its monies are to be spent."[47] Black women[48] and other minority women are also represented in greater numbers at lower levels. Human service organizations have increased their number of minority employees in recent years but still have a long way to go. The complexion of policymaking, planning, and implementation is predominantly that of a certain race and sex, but class and age enter in as well. Most minorities working in human service organizations that serve the minority aged are not within the same economic class as the minority aged being served. It is worth stating here that there "is simply no conclusive evidence, however, that a counselor must experience everything his/her client does."[49] Still, this is a factor that must be considered. It could be argued that those minorities which have participated in activist organizations, such as the Welfare Rights Organization, have not been completely shunted aside from some kind of input into policymaking and planning. But the minority aged as a whole have very little input into social policies or plans that affect them. Low-income minority aged are virtually without a voice in the entire social policy picture.

Most human service organizations that profess to serve the needs of the minority aged are bureaucratic organizations. The rational legal form of bureaucracy developed over many centuries in Western civilization, grew slowly since the Middle Ages, and reached its full form on a widespread basis in the twentieth century.[50] The noted work of Max Weber has described and analyzed the transition of Western society from the patriarchal, feudal, traditional system of the Middle Ages to the modern rationalization and bureaucratization of modern society.[51] "Tocqueville was one of the very first nineteenth-century social thinkers to become seriously interested in the problem of bureaucracy," states Nisbet. "That is, the problem created for free societies by the constant expansion of political administrations, with formalized, paid, permanent bureaucracies performing duties that had previously been performed by one or another of the social groups composing society."[52] In a sense the tendency for social policies to be universalistic rather than particular in purview goes hand in hand with the nature of bureaucratization itself. Both conjoin to cause difficulty for the formulation of an ethnically conscious, transcultural aging policy.

Most criticisms of bureaucracy fall into one of two camps.[53] The first would emphasize the apparent inflexibility, inefficiency, unresponsiveness, and lack of creativity of bureaucracies. The second criticism focuses on the perceived effects of bureaucracies on the employees themselves, such as the possible stifling of spontaneity, freedom, and self-realization. On both counts the minority aged are in a disadvantageous position. Even learning about how to deal with modern social service bureaucracies can and is a considerable problem for many white "professionals" (many with advanced degrees). Many minority aged have limited formal education. Some are illiterate or cannot speak English. As has been stated previously, 5 percent of the older population does not speak English; of that 5 percent, 30 percent speak Spanish, 20 percent Italian, with the remainder speaking a number of other languages.[54] Most English speakers do not speak the language well. Hence, language problems alone, coupled with the labyrinthine information networks of modern bureaucracies are enough to deter many from seeking services.

Almost by nature social service bureaucracies are not as responsive as they could be to the particular needs of minority aged. Bureaucracies are, at the very least, a product of the dominant culture or cultures of a given society (referring to the discussion on this topic in the first chapter of the book). The minority aged are "different" from the mainstream, and bureaucracies have historically had a difficult time coping with differences. Indeed, Michael Novak has argued that the "fact of American cultural power is that a more or less upper class, Northeastern Protestant sensibility sets the tone, and that a fairly aggressive British American ethnocentricity, and even Anglophilia, govern the instruments of education and public life."[55] Hence other white ethnic cultures and experiences have been shunted aside in favor of a larger British-American bias and orientation. This is in no way to suggest that white ethnics and minority peoples of color have received anything like the same kind of treatment, only to argue that important differences within white cultures (Polish-American, Irish-American, Jewish-American, etc.) are often not recognized by bureaucratic organizations or in policy formulation and implementation.

Bureaucratic organizations that serve the minority aged must cope with the considerable variety of subcultures within minority cultures in general. For example, there are four different Hispanic subgroups, several subgroups among the black population, eighteen distinct subgroups of Asian Americans, and 288 North American Indian tribes.[56] Within each subgroup there are differences in culture, linguistic expression, etc. Even within that context there are further human personality variables that need to be considered.[57] Indeed, the diversity is so great even within one ethnic group so as to make virtually meaningless at times a group lumping such as the Chicano aged, or the Hispanic aged.[58] Interestingly, a Puerto Rican elderly woman in New York and a Mexican-American elderly woman in the Rio Grande Valley of Texas have different cultures, experiences, and linguistic modes and expressions. Yet a national aging policy must attempt in some way to attune to the needs of both. Yet at the same time there are shared elements (probably more shared elements than particularistic elements), which a national aging policy must address and emphasize. Bureaucratic organizations have a seeming legal and social mandate to treat everyone the same, and yet everyone is not the same. The notion that everyone is not the same is perhaps more true in America than in almost any other country. Yet policies and bureaucratic organizations would appear to pull and tug the minority aged (and perhaps all ethnic aged) in the direction of sameness. This pull and tug springs partly, of course, from the nature of policies and bureaucratic organizations in general and partly from the fact that to a great extent "cultural concerns were not highlighted at the very beginning of the federal thrust in aging. It was only in the beginning of the seventies that there was a glimmer of hope for any identifiable emphasis on cultural differences or similarities."[59]

Professionals and paraprofessionals working in human service organizations quickly become adapted to a prevailing bureaucratic ethos. Interestingly, minority professionals often react in similarly bureaucratic, professional, rational ways to the needs of minority aged recipients of services. Sometimes minority recipients of services may respond with anger when confronted with a minority counselor,[60] associating the minority counselor as merely a mouthpiece for white controlled institutions and culture. Sometimes minority professionals adopt the same white stereotypes of minority clients.[61] Sometimes minority professionals working with minority-aged clients of another culture do not have a good understanding of that culture. An example might be a black human service professional working with a Hispanic elderly person or a Hispanic human service professional working with a black elderly person. Class enters in as well. The culture of a white lower-class elderly person may in some ways be as foreign to a middle-class white professional as the black or chicano cultures may conceivably be. Linguistic differences cut across race lines, ethnic lines, and class lines. The most obvious linguistic differences are that many Hispanic aged speak English either very haltingly or else not at all. Beyond this, there are linguistic differences within each language group (Puerto Rican Spanish and Cuban Spanish) and social class (English spoken by lower-class white elderly and English spoken by middle- and upper-class white elderly). In addition, cultural implications of nonverbal behavior[62] are seminal, particularly with the Indian elderly.

Perspectives and insights from sociolinguistics and psycholinguistics, gerontological anthropology,[63] cross-cultural psychology,[64] transcultural psychiatry,[65] transcultural nursing,[66] social work,[67] and other disciplines and professions can be helpful in aiding policymaking and human service bureaucratic agencies and organizations in becoming more conscious and responsive to cultural differences. Policies, services, programs, and organizations exist in a society with cultural differences, differences that must be respected and honored. If these cultural differences are not respected and honored, then the minority-aged recipients of services have much to lose, and indeed the rest of society as well.

WORKING FOR CHANGE IN AGING SERVICES WITH AND ON BEHALF OF AGED MINORITY CONSUMERS

This chapter began on somewhat of a political note and perforce must to a certain extent end on a political note. The "making of collective decisions in a world of conflicting values is the chief task of politics."[68] Indeed, conflicting values are very much at play in the America of the 1980s. Several notions are advanced here in respect to working for change in aging services with and on behalf of minority-aged consumers. There is no pretense here that these recommendations are all inclusive nor that they are equally applicable to all times, places, and societies. However, they seem relevant and worthy of discussion as possible avenues of approach now.

Certainly a prelude to change making of any kind, indeed the ultimate aim of public debate and decision making, is that of mature judgments on the best courses of action to take.[69] Behind mature judgments rests some kind of reasonably coherent personal social and political philosophy. Thought precedes action, certainly. In this regard, thought must be informed by good social philosophy,[70] and considered ethical,[71] social justice,[72] and theological perspectives.[73] This is not to argue that one must be an intellectual or a theoretician or have read everything on the above areas before acting in any way, but simply to underscore Alinsky's remark that the most commonly asked, pervasive question of any agent for social change is the question "Why?"[74] This is not to argue that answers here are easily forthcoming or perhaps even possible. Indeed, Tracy argues that "philosophical and theological perspectives do not ordinarily provide specific solutions to specific questions but rather general value-orientations in the search for specific solutions."[75]

The political context of minority aging is seminal. Political decisions are being made now and will continue to be made in the years

to come that affect the minority aged in momentous ways. Therefore, our first recommendation must be that of political action. Two
current political developments are informative here: (a) movement
of social policy decisions back to the states and local areas and (b)
budgetary cutbacks and limitations in social programs and social
policies as a whole. The economic and political assumptions currently in vogue are based on supply-side economic arguments that emphasize economic growth and economic productivity as the perceived remedy or partial remedy for social problems.

Political action and advocacy for the minority aged will probably
be most effective in the future at the local and state level. Since decision making will be increasingly taking place at that level, it would
behoove the change agent to direct many of his or her efforts at that
level. Alinsky and a number of others have traditionally argued for
the initiation of change efforts from the ground level upward; this
means joining and becoming involved in citizen action groups; this
means knowing the views of one's state representative, state senator,
or city councilperson and attempting to wield influence on behalf of
the aged and the minority aged. While most citizens may never
originate legislation, it is very possible to have an important, even
decisive, influence on its passage or rejection.[76] Well-researched,
well-written letters are one way. Another way is a visit to the office of
the state representative or state senator (or city councilperson) in the
area in which one resides to discuss a given piece of legislation affecting the minority aged or to discuss one's views in general in this or
other areas. Sometimes it is helpful to first contact the staff person
who has staff responsibility in that given area (social legislation or
aging legislation, etc.). Staff people do have influence themselves,
and such a contact can be most helpful and advantageous.

Involvement in a political party can be effective. In recent years
political parties have been said to have only been marginally effective instruments, and calls have been made for their revival.[77]
Political parties do have some influence, particularly at certain in-
tersecting points in the political arena. An individual working for
change on behalf of the minority aged might become involved in
various party meetings and activities, perhaps becoming a candidate
for a particular party position. Advocacy groups, such as the League
of United Latin American Citizens and the National Association for
the Advancement of Colored People, can be effective instruments for

change.

Above all, an individual working for change should become thoroughly acquainted with and have analyzed the important issues in aging policy. Many of these issues "have appeared and re-appeared in various ways, under various labels, for decades."[78] What might be the possibilities of a more adequately cast transcultural perspective of many of the social programs serving the minority aged? Any possible answer to that question cannot possibly be formulated outside the context of an in-depth analysis of the policy issues that rest at the base or core of programs serving the minority aged, of the socioeconomic system that underlies these policy issues, and of ways of affecting change in that system.

A second avenue of approach in respect to working for change in these areas is to focus one's efforts on the human service organizations that serve the minority aged. How can human service bureaucratic organizations serving the minority aged become more responsive and creative in respect to serving the minority aged? Problems in this area have been explored earlier in this chapter. Solutions, as in most areas of the human services, are often elusive and seldom acquired easily; however, there are possibilities.

Certainly citizen participation is one place to start. The minority aged need to have a voice in what goes on in the human service organizations that purport to serve them. An area agency on aging might be a good place to begin. How many minority aged serve on the advisory committee to the area agency on aging (an advisory committee is required)? Of those minority aged who do serve, how much real participation takes place? How well informed are the minority aged about the agency, its activities, and beyond that, the possibilities in respect to their increased participation?

A useful perspective here is the societal learning or social learning approach. I prefer the term societal learning over social learning so that it is not confused with social learning theory (behaviorism). Developed by Friedman[79] and also Dunn, Schon, Hampden-Turner, and others,[80] the societal learning approach conceives of planning as a form of learning, moving in the direction of a highly learning oriented citizen participation. The policymaker and the citizen participant both participate in a mutual learning process, whereby the experiential knowledge of the citizen and the abstracted, processed knowledge of the planner are merged or fused through extensive dialogue and interchange. The world of the agency, the agency professional, programs, and services delivered by the agency, etc., are confusing and bewildering to many minority-aged consumers. These approaches may be helpful in respect to encouraging the aged citizen participant in the direction of real participation.

Language problems of many minority aged only increase the amount of bewilderment that they experience. Perhaps an appropriate target for change would be the way that agencies convey information about their programs to the minority aged. It is often not enough to simply translate bureaucratic English into bureaucratic Spanish for many of the Hispanic aged. Indeed bureaucratic Spanish can seemingly resemble another language to many of the Hispanic aged. Other minority aged also have problems with agency languages. Perhaps a minority aged citizen participant could be of immense help to an agency in respect to translating agency programs into the everyday language spoken by the minority elderly consumers of these services in the locale served. This is to take nothing away from the need for the necessity for minority aged of all ethnic groups to have an adequate knowledge of English by which they can cope at least a little more effectively with the complex demands of the knowledge society. Indeed, social welfare approaches that do not at the same time attempt to provide sound training in English for the minority aged who have difficulty with same only in effect segregate the minority aged still further and also assuredly reinforce poverty conditions by so doing. However, programs, services, and organizations need to begin where the minority aged person is at, culturally, linguistically, and personally.

Transportation is an immense problem for the minority aged,[81] and an agent for change would do well to recognize *why* it is such a problem. The same socioeconomic system that has dictated lower incomes for the minority aged also has something to do with services as well. Only a coordinated, comprehensive mass transportation system makes any kind of long-range sense. To effect such a system requires political activity of a larger order (certainly without a coordinated means of transportation the minority aged cannot get to services and services cannot be delivered to them).

Health, mental health, housing, transportation: The needs are great and seemingly limitless in respect to the minority aged.

Change agents can find appropriate areas in which to work for change within human service organizations with and on behalf of the minority aged. It may be in the area of persuading a mental health agency to be more open to the use of curanderos in working with Chicanos[82]; it may be in working to persuade a social service agency to hire more minority counselors or administrators; and it may be in countless other areas.

Sound qualitative and quantitative research is needed with respect to policies, programs, and human service organizations serving the needs of minority aged. Need assessment is a crucial and much needed element with respect to this overall process.[83] Traditionally, policymakers have tended to slight qualitative research. Yet parallel to this there has been a seeming increase in recent years in the amount of criticism concerning the available quantitative research for policymaking, some focusing on the positivistic nature of the research[84] and others on the lack of policy relevance of the research and other aspects. Qualitative research has perhaps been given new life in recent years with the input of phenomenological perspectives and by ethnomethodology.[85] Ethnomethodology may have much to offer in respect to providing a better understanding of the minority aged, for it purports to go inside social scenes and examine the phenomena from the actor's perspective or point of view.[86] This kind of research is needed (in addition to sound quantitative research) for the perspectives and points of view of the minority aged themselves need to come out in the study or research, (and in policies, programs, and in human service organizations as well). Another kind of qualitative approach (mentioned by Simić) that might serve as a useful tool in studying the needs of the minority aged is the life history approach.[87]

All the studies that could be made concerning the needs of the minority aged would certainly agree on one seminal item: The minority aged need a higher average income level than they now have. Income inequality is an obvious and sad fact of life, and the minority aged are rather dramatic examples of these inequalities. Working for change here, working for a more equalitarian society, should be the fulcrum point of any change effort on behalf of the minority aged. An adequate income floor for all aged is the foundation stone upon which any transcultural aging policy or program can be constructed. Supplementary Security Income (S.S.I.) is at least a small first step in this direction. Certainly transcultural perspectives on aging policies have much to do with notions of identity, personhood, and belonging. However, identity, personhood, and belonging can only legitimately be couched within a strong context of basic income and social *security*.

This commitment to income and social *security* can only be achieved through larger philosophical and societal commitments to equalitarian ends. However, supply-side economic theorists and others are right in their argument that the welfare state, social services, and social programs can only be supported by economic productivity. In short, it takes large amounts of monies and economic productivity to support large-scale aging policies and programs. It is within that context that a future emphasis in aging policy will be placed on the needs of the frail elderly and the elderly in general will be asked to stay in the work force for a longer period of time. Our concern in expanding social services that can meet the many needs of the minority aged and all aged is also a concern with increasing productivity in society, since both are so intimately conjoined (Great Britain is a notable example of problems in this area).

There has been increasing concern in recent years with social change efforts directed at the economic structure or system itself. There is not so much talk of ideological stances or movements, socialism, for example, as with democratizing capitalism (and socialism). Indeed, social change efforts have taken a definite democratic turn. There is much discussion of the notion of economic democracy.[88] This has much to offer in respect to change efforts on behalf of the minority aged. Advocates of this approach would like to ensure more input into decision making on behalf of workers and indeed on behalf of all citizens of a reputedly democratic society. The emergence of the Solidarity movement in Poland may be one example of this kind of thinking. Democratic involvement of minority workers in economic decision making is important, for at the very least it may help to ensure a better present and future for minorities. For those minority aged who are now not part of the formal work force, there are numerous other opportunities for democracy to take root. Certainly the encouragement of active citizen participation of low-income aged by area agencies on aging and other agencies in the field of aging (discussed earlier) is one important place to start.[89]

Aging policies and services that are oriented in a transcultural direction are designed in such a way as to recognize differences and respond to differences. There should be a flexibility and an openness to change in the human service organizations that carry out these policies because of the nature of cultural variations that are discussed in this book. Social policies, programs, and institutions need to be at least as intricately tuned, particular, and change-conscious as the complex cultures of the minority aged they are designed to serve. Indeed, policies, programs, and institutions need to be cross-culturally oriented and anthropologically informed[90] (and informed by other disciplines and professions as well) to even begin to encounter the considerable complexity of cultures, such as varied minority-aged cultures, on an equal footing.

REFERENCES

1. Clark, Margaret, and Anderson, Barbara Gallatin: *Culture and Aging: An Anthropological Study of Older Americans.* Springfield, Illinois, Thomas, 1967, p.3.
2. Herskovits, M.J.: *Man and His Works: The Science of Cultural Anthropology.* New York, Knopf, 1948, p.17.
3. Novak, Michael: *Further Reflections on Ethnicity.* Middletown, Pennsylvania, EMPAC, Jednota Press, 1977, p. 19; see also Novak, Michael: *The Rise of the Unmeltable Ethnics.* New York, Macmillan, 1972; Mindel, C.H., and Habenstein, R.W. (Eds.): *Ethnic Families in America,* 2nd ed. New York, Elsevier North-Holland, 1981 (first edition published in 1976); Mindel, C.H., and Markides, K.S.: *Older People and Their Families: Relationships and Transitions.* New York, Springer, in press; Markides, K.S.; and Mindel, C.H.: *Cross-Cultural Aging in America.* St. Louis, C.V. Mosby, in press.
4. Federal Council on the Aging, *Policy Issues Concerning the Elderly Minorities, A Staff Report.* Washington, Department of Health and Human Services, Federal Council on the Aging, 1979.
5. Nozick, Robert: *Anarchy, State and Utopia.* New York, Basic Books, 1974.
6. Novak, Michael (Ed.): *The Denigration of Capitalism: Six Points of View.* Washington, American Enterprise Institute for Public Policy Research, 1979; Novak, Michael: *The American Vision: An Essay on the Future of Democratic Capitalism.* Washington, American Enterprise Institute for Public Policy Research, 1978; Novak, Michael (Ed.): *Democracy and Mediating Structures: A Theological Enquiry.* Washington, American Enterprise Institute for Public Policy Research, 1980.
7. Gilder, George: *Wealth and Poverty.* New York, Basic Books, 1980.
8. Sowell, Thomas: *Classical Economics Reconsidered.* Princeton, New Jersey, Princeton University Press, 1974; *Race and Economics.* New York, Longman, 1975; *Affirmative Action Reconsidered: Was It Necessary in Academia?* Washington, American Enterprise Institute, 1975; *Knowledge and Decisions.* New York, Basic

Books, 1980; *Markets and Minorities.* New York, Basic Books, 1981.

9. Rawls, John: *A Theory of Justice.* Cambridge, Harvard University Press, 1971.
10. Hudson, Robert B.: Old-age politics in a period of change. In Borgatta, Edgar F., and McCluskey, Neil G. (Eds.): *Aging and Society: Current Research and Policy Perspectives.* Beverly Hills, California, Sage, 1980, p.156.
11. Estes, Carroll L.: *The Aging Enterprise.* San Francisco, Jossey-Bass, 1979.
12. U.S. Congress, Senate: *Developments in Aging,* part 1. A report of the Special Committee on Aging, 1978, 95th Congress, 2nd session, Chapter 2, pp. 31-41.
13. Freeman, Roger: *The Wayward Welfare State.* Palo Alto, Hoover Institution Press, 1981.
14. Steinfels, Peter: *The Neoconservatives: The Men Who Are Changing America's Politics.* New York, Simon and Schuster, 1979, p. 59.
15. Logue, John: The welfare state: Victim of its success. *Daedalus, 108:*78, 1979.
16. U.S. Department of Health and Human Services, Administration on Aging: *Characteristics of the Black Elderly — 1980: Statistical Reports on Older Americans.* Washington, U.S. Department of Health and Human Services, Administration on Aging, 1980, p. 4; see also U.S. Bureau of the Census: *Statistical Abstract of the United States: 1980*(101st edition). Washington, U.S. Government Printing Office, 1980, p. 29; see also U.S. Bureau of the Census and the Administration on Aging: *Guide to Census Data on the Elderly.* Washington, U.S. Government Printing Office, 1978.
17. U.S. Bureau of the Census, Current Population Reports, Series P-20, No. 363, *Population Profile of the United States, 1980.* U.S. Government Printing Office, Washington, D.C., 1981.
18. Lowy, Louis: *Social Policies and Programs on Aging.* Lexington, Massachusetts, Lexington Books, 1980, p. 17.
19. Siegel, Jacob S.: Demographic aspects of aging in the United States. In Ostfeld, Adrian, and Gibson, Don C., (Eds): *Epidemiology of Aging.* Washington, Public Health Service, n.d., pp. 34-51.
20. U.S. Department of Health, Education and Welfare: Some prospects for the future elderly population. *Statistical Reports on Older Populations,* No. 3. Washington, Administration on Aging, 1978, p. 11.
21. Pavalko, Ron: The 1980 census: How to find the numbers that count. *The Grantsmanship Center News, 8:*30, 1980.
22. Bengtson, Vern L.: Ethnicity and aging: Problems and issues in current social science inquiry. In Gelfand, Donald E., and Kutzik, Alfred J. (Eds.): *Ethnicity and Aging: Theory, Research, and Policy.* New York, Springer, 1979, p. 13.
23. U.S. Bureau of the Census, Current Population Reports P-60, No. 127, *Money Income and Poverty Status of Families and Persons in the United States: 1980* (Advance Data from the March 1981 Current Population Survey). U.S. Government Printing Office, Washington, D.C., 1981.
24. Lindsay, I.B.: *The Multiple Hazards of Age and Race: The Situation of Aged Blacks in the United States.* Washington, U.S. Government Printing Office, 1971.
25. Jackson, Jacquelyne J.: Social Impacts of housing relocation upon urban, low-income Black aged. *Gerontologist, 12:*32-37, 1972.
26. Jackson, Jacquelyne J.: *Minorities and Aging.* Belmont, California, Wadsworth,

1980, p. 164.

27. Ball, Robert M.: *Social Security: Today and Tomorrow.* New York, Columbia University Press, 1978.

28. National Urban League: *Double Jeopardy: The Older Negro in America Today.* Washington, National Urban League, 1964; Henderson, George: The Negro recipient of old-age assistance: Results of discrimination. *Social Casework, 46*:208-214, 1965.

29. Cowgill, Donald O., and Holmes, Lowell D. (Eds.): *Aging and Modernization.* New York, Appleton-Century-Crofts, 1972.

30. National Council on Aging: *Triple Jeopardy: Myth or Reality.* Washington, National Council on Aging, 1972.

31. Sterne, Richard S., Phillips, James, and Rabuska, A.: *The Urban Elderly Poor.* Lexington, Massachusetts, Heath, 1974; Cantor, Marjorie H.: Effect of ethnicity on life styles of the inner city elderly. In Lawton, M.P., Newcomer, R.J., and Byerts, T.O. (Eds.): *Community Planning for an Aging Society.* Stroudsburg, Pennsylvania, Dowden, Hutchinson and Ross, 1976, pp. 41-58.

32. Shank, Robert E.: Nutrition and aging. In Ostfeld, Adrian, and Gibson, Don C. (Eds.): *Epidemiology of Aging.* Washington, Public Health Service, n.d., pp. 199-213.

33. Cantor, Marjorie, H.: The informal support system of New York's inner city elderly: Is ethnicity a factor? In Gelfand, Donald E., and Kutzik, Alfred J. (Eds.): *Ethnicity and Aging: Theory, Research and Policy.* New York, Springer, 1979, p. 154.

34. Maldonado, Jr., David: Aging in the Chicano context. In Gelfand, Donald E., and Kutzik, Alfred J. (Eds.): *Ethnicity and Aging: Theory, Research and Policy.* New York, Springer, 1979, p. 179.

35. Murrillo, Nathan: The Mexican-American family. In Martinez, Ricardo Arguijo (Ed.): *Hispanic Culture and Health Care: Fact, Fiction, Folklore.* St. Louis, Mosby, 1978, pp. 3-18. See also the second edition (1980).

36. Wilson, William Julius: *The Declining Significance of Race.* Chicago, University of Chicago Press, 1978.

37. The Black plight — Race or class? A debate between Kenneth B. Clark and Carl Gershman. *The New York Times Magazine,* October 5, 1980, pp. 22-33, 90-109.

38. Galper, Jeffrey: *The Politics of Social Services.* Englewood Cliffs, New Jersey, Prentice-Hall, 1978; Galpher, Jeffrey: *Social Work Practice: A Radical Perspective.* Englewood Cliffs, New Jersey, Prentice-Hall, 1980; Harvey, David: *Social Justice and the City.* Baltimore, Johns Hopkins, 1973.

39. Pettigrew, Thomas F. (Ed.): *The Sociology of Race Relations: Reflection and Reform.* New York, Free Press, 1980, p. 317.

40. Barrera, Mario: *Race and Class in the Southwest: A Theory of Racial Inequality.* Notre Dame, University of Notre Dame Press, 1979; Watts, Thomas D.: Mario Barrera's left internal colonial model: A theory of racial inequality in the southwest (review essay of *Race and Class in the Southwest: A Theory of Racial Inequality,* by Mario Barrera). In *The Borderlands Journal* (published by the South Texas Institute of Latin and Mexican-American Research), *3*:195-199, 1980.

41. Gordon, Milton M.: *Assimilation in American Life.* New York, Oxford, 1964; Gordon, Milton M.: *Human Nature, Class, and Ethnicity.* New York, Oxford, 1978.
42. Parsons, Talcott: *Structure and Process in Modern Societies.* Glencoe, Illinois, Free Press, 1960, p. 17.
43. Huttman, Elizabeth D.: *Introduction to Social Policy.* New York, McGraw-Hill, 1981, p. 5.
44. Morris, Robert: *Social Policy of the American Welfare State: An Introduction to Policy Analysis.* New York, Harper and Row, 1979, p. 1.
45. Kahn, Alfred J.: *Social Policy and Social Services,* 2nd edition. New York, Random House, 1979, p. 8.
46. Margulies, Newton, and Wallace, John: *Organizational Change: Techniques and Applications.* Glenview, Illinois, Scott, Foresman and Co., 1973, p. 44.
47. Norman, Elaine, and Mancuso, Arlene: Introduction. In Norman, Elaine, and Mancuso, Arlene (Eds): *Women's Issues and Social Work Practice.* Itasca, Illinois, F.E. Peacock, 1980, p. 4.
48. Joseph, Barbara: Ain't I a woman. In Norman, Elaine, and Mancuso, Arlene (Eds.): *Women's Issues and Social Work Practice.* Itasca, Illinois, F.E. Peacock, 1980, pp. 91-111.
49. Atkinson, Donald R., Morten, George, and Sue, Derald Wing: Minority group counseling: An overview. In Atkinson, Donald R., Morten, George, and Sue, Derald Wing (Eds.): *Counseling American Minorities: A Cross-Cultural Perspective.* Dubuque, William C. Brown Co., 1979, p. 23.
50. Bendix, Reinhard: Bureaucracy. In *International Encyclopedia of the Social Sciences.* New York, The Free Press, 1977.
51. Weber, Max: *The Theory of Social and Economic Organization.* Henderson, A.M., and Parsons, Talcott, trans., and eds. New York, Oxford, 1947, and other works by Weber.
52. Nisbet, Robert: *The Social Philosophers: Community and Conflict in Western Thought.* New York: Crowell, 1973, p. 424.
53. Perrow, Charles: *Complex Organizations: A Critical Essay.* Glenview, Illinois, Scott, Foresman and Co., 1979, p. 6.
54. U.S. Department of Health, Education, and Welfare: Some prospects for the future elderly population. *Statistical Reports on Older Americans,* No. 3. Washington, Administration on Aging, 1978, p. 11.
55. Novak, Michael: *Further Reflections on Ethnicity.* Middletown, Pennsylvania, Jednota Press, 1977, pp. 13-14.
56. U.S. Department of Health, Education, and Welfare, Administration on Aging: *The Minority Elderly in America: An Annotated Bibliography.* Washington, U.S. Department of Health and Human Services, Administration on Aging, 1980, p. 1.
57. Levine, Elaine S., and Padilla, Amado M.: *Crossing Cultures in Therapy: Pluralistic Counseling for the Hispanic.* Monterey, California, Brooks/Cole, Division of Wadsworth, 1980, pp. 1-19.
58. Watts, Thomas D.: *Social Policy and the Aged: Transcultural Perspectives.* Paper delivered at the Southern Anthropological Society, 16th Annual Meeting,

April 2, 1981, Fort Worth, Texas.

59. Stanford, E. Percil: Service delivery concerns from a minority aged perspective: The Black aged. In Wright, Roosevelt (Ed.): *Black/Chicano Elderly: Service Delivery within a Cultural Context — Proceedings of the First Annual Symposium on the Black/Chicano Elderly.* Arlington, Texas, Graduate School of Social Work, The University of Texas at Arlington, 1980, p. 35.

60. Jackson, A.M.: Psychotherapy: Factors associated with the race of the therapist. *Psychotherapy: Theory, Research and Practice, 10*:273-277, 1973.

61. Calnek, M.: Racial factors in the countertransference: The Black therapist and the Black client. *American Journal of Orthopsychiatry, 40*:39-46, 1970.

62. Wolfgang, Aaron (Ed.): *Nonverbal Behavior: Applications and Cultural Implications.* New York, Academic Press, 1979.

63. Fry, Christine L. (Ed.): *Dimensions: Aging, Culture, and Health.* New York, Praeger, 1981; Fry, Christine L. (Ed.): *Aging in Culture and Society: Comparative Viewpoints and Strategies.* New York, Bergin, 1980; see also Simmons, Leo: *The Role of the Aged in Primitive Society.* New Haven, Yale University Press, 1945; Clark, Margaret and Anderson, Barbara G.: *Culture and Aging: An Anthropological Study of Older Americans.* Springfield, Illinois, Thomas, 1967.

64. Segall, Marshall H.: *Cross-Cultural Psychology: Human Behavior in Global Perspective.* Monterey, California, Brooks/Cole, Division of Wadsworth, 1979; Warren, Neil (Ed.): *Studies in Cross-Cultural Psychology.* New York, Academic Press, 1977; Triandis, H.C. (Ed.): *Handbook of Cross-Cultural Psychology* (6 vols.). Boston, Allyn and Bacon, 1979. The following two journals publish articles in this area (among others): *Journal of Cross-Cultural Psychology* (1970, founded) and the *International Journal of Psychology* (1966, founded).

65. Draguns, J.G., and Phillips, L.: *Culture and Psychopathology: The Quest for a Relationship.* Morristown, General Learning Press, 1972.

66. Leininger, Madeleine M.: *Transcultural Nursing: Concepts, Theories and Practices.* New York, Wiley, 1978.

67. Norton, Dolores G.: *The Dual Perspective: Inclusion of Ethnic Minority Content in the Social Work Curriculum.* New York, Council on Social Work Education, 1978; Mizio, Emelicia (Ed.): *Puerto Rican Task Force Report: Project on Ethnicity.* New York, Family Service Association of America, 1979, and others; Schwartz, Florence: *A Cross-Cultural Encounter: A Non-Traditional Approach to Social Work Education.* San Francisco, R and E Research Associates, 1977.

68. Gordon, Scott: *Welfare, Justice, and Freedom.* New York, Columbia University Press, 1980, p. 47.

69. McKenna, George, and Feingold, Stanley (Eds.): *Taking Sides: Clashing Views on Controversial Issues.* Guilford, Connecticut, Dushkin, 1978, p. xix; see also Massialas, Byron G., Sprague, Nancy F., and Hurst, Joseph B.: *Social Issues Through Inquiry: Coping in an Age of Crisis.* Englewood Cliffs, New Jersey, Prentice-Hall, 1975.

70. Feinberg, Joel: *Social Philosophy.* Englewood Cliffs, New Jersey, Prentice-Hall, 1973.

71. Neugarten, Bernice L., and Havighurst, Robert J. (Eds.): *Social Policy, Social Ethnics, and the Aging Society.* Washington, U.S. Government Printing Office,

1976. *See especially* Diggs, B.J.: The ethics of providing for the economic well-being of the aged; Morgan, James N.: The ethical basis of the economic claims of the elderly; Jonsen, Albert R., S.J.: Principles for an ethics of health services; and other articles in this volume.

72. Fenton, Thomas P. (Ed.): *Education for Justice: A Resource Manual.* Maryknoll, New York, Orbis, 1975, and others; Kelbley, Charles A. (Ed.): *The Value of Justice: Essays on the Theory and Practice of Social Virtue.* New York, Fordham University Press, 1979.

73. Hiltner, Seward (Ed.): *Toward a Theology of Aging.* New York, Human Sciences Press, 1975, and others.

74. Alinsky, Saul: *Reveille for Radicals.* New York, Vintage-Random House, 1969, p. xiii (Orig. Publ. in 1946).

75. Tracy, David: Eschatological perspectives on aging. In Hiltner, Seward (Ed.): *Toward a Theology of Aging.* New York, Human Sciences Press, 1975, p. 134.

76. Wright, Jim (Congressman): *You and Your Congressman,* rev. ed. New York, Capricorn Books, G.P. Putnam's Sons, 1976, p. 206.

77. Pomper, Gerald M.: *Voter's Choice: Varieties of American Electoral Behavior.* New York, Harper and Row, 1975, pp. 210-226.

78. Miller, Warren E., and Levitin, Teresa E.: *Leadership and Change: The New Politics and the American Electorate.* Cambridge, Massachusetts, Winthrop, 1976, p. 11.

79. Friedman, John, and Hudson, Barclay: Knowledge and action: A guide to planning theory. *Journal of the American Institute of Planners, 40*:2-16, 1974; Friedman, John: *Retracking America: A Guide to Transactive Planning.* Garden City, New York, Doubleday, 1973; Friedman, John: *The Good Society.* Cambridge, Massachusetts, MIT Press, 1979.

80. Dunn, Edgar, S.: *Economic and Social Development: A Process of Social Learning.* Baltimore, Johns Hopkins Press, 1971; Schon, Donald A.: *Beyond the Stable State.* New York, Norton, 1971; Hampden-Turner, Charles: *Radical Man: The Process of Psycho-Social Development.* Garden City, New York, Anchor Books/Doubleday and Co., 1970, etc.; see also Watts, Thomas D.: *The Societal Learning Approach: A New Approach to Social Welfare Policy and Planning in America.* Saratoga, California, Century Twenty One Publ., Division of R and E Res. Assoc., 1981.

81. Cornehls, James V., and Taebel, Del A.: The outsiders and urban transportation. *Social Science Journal, 13*:61-73, 1976.

82. Clark, M. Margaret: *Health in the Mexican American Culture.* Berkeley and Los Angeles, University of California Press, 1959; *Curanderismo: The Art of Folk Healing and Its Implications for the Hispanic Elderly.* Conference presented by the Center for Chicano Aged and the Graduate School of Social Work, The University of Texas at Arlington, June 17, 1981, Arlington, Texas.

83. Wright, Roosevelt: Assessing the needs of the minority aged: Methodologies and techniques. In Wright, Roosevelt (Ed.): *Black/Chicano Elderly: Service Delivery Within a Cultural Context — Proceedings of the First Annual Symposium on the Black/Chicano Elderly.* Arlington, Texas, Graduate School of Social Work, The University of Texas at Arlington, 1980, pp. 63-69.

84. Lindblom, Charles E., and Cohen, David K.: *Usable Knowledge: Social Science and Social Problem-Solving.* New Haven, Yale University Press, 1979.
85. Garfinkel, Harold: *Studies in Ethnomethodology.* Englewood Cliffs, New Jersey, Prentice-Hall, 1967; Attewell, Paul: Ethnomethodology since Garfinkel. *Theory and Society,* *1*:179-210, 1974; Watts, Thomas D.: Ethnomethodology. In Grinnell, Jr., Richard (Ed.) *Social Work Research and Evaluation.* Itasca, Illinois, F.E. Peacock, 1981, pp. 361-372.
86. Ramos, Reyes: A case in point: An ethnomethodological study of a poor Mexican American family. *Social Science Quarterly, 53*:905-919, 1973; Ramos, Reyes, Being old and being a minority: The double whammy. In Wright, Jr., Roosevelt (Ed.): *Black/Chicano Elderly: Service Delivery Within a Cultural Context — Proceedings of the First Annual Symposium on the Black/Chicano Elderly.* Arlington, Texas, Graduate School of Social Work, The University of Texas at Arlington, 1980, pp. 79-82.
87. Simić, Andrei: Aging and the aged in cultural perspective. In Myerhoff, Barbara G., and Simić, Andrei (Eds.): *Life's Career-Aging: Cultural Variations on Growing Old.* Beverly Hills, California, Sage, 1978, p. 21.
88. Carnoy, Martin, and Shearer, Derek: *Economic Democracy: The Challenge of the 1980s.* Armonk, New York, M.E. Sharpe, Inc., 1980.
89. Watts, Thomas D.: *Citizen Participation of Low Income Aged: The Contributions of the Societal Learning Approach.* Paper delivered at the Southwest Society on Aging, Third Annual Conference, September 30, 1981, Tulsa, Oklahoma.
90. Cochrane, Glynn: Policy studies and anthropology. *Current Anthropology, 21*:445-458, 1980.

Chapter 4

THE TRANSCULTURAL PERSPECTIVE AND HEALTH AND MENTAL HEALTH SERVICES

HEALTH and mental health issues and concerns cannot be easily separated from larger social, political, and economic trends and changes. For example in the late 1970s and to now, two major trends have had and will continue to have serious reverberations in our ideas and policies toward health care. The first is what seems to be a declining interest in the poor and minorities of color as publics of concern and an eruption of concern with oneself and one's family. The second is the continuing and fluctuating tension between inflation and recession (stagflation).[1] As far as health care is concerned, in the first instance we made great strides as a nation in the 1960s in providing a significant degree of governmental support for health care for the indigent and aged (Medicaid and Medicare) as a part of what appeared as a general concern for the plight of those with insufficient resources. Today, the main concern is spreading the high cost of illness and its treatment around for all to share, to raise the productivity of health service delivery, to reduce federal involvement, and to encourage local governments and the private sector to increase their involvement, moral and fiscal.[2] In the latter case, while inflation continues to erode the value of the dollar, the cost of medical care skyrockets and continues to inflate at a rate virtually unmatched in any other sector of American life.

Americans have always seemed concerned, however naively or egoistically, with their health. This concern (preoccupation, perhaps) has not necessarily been translated into a rational system of health care or even a very rational use of the health care system that exists. In addition, it has resulted in the profusion of a variety of alternative modes of caring for and thinking about health (both physical and mental health), alternatives that range from sheer quackery to legitimate and time-honored methods of approaching the problem of illness. As health care stretches out of reach of more and more of our population, especially the poor and marginally

93

comfortable, we can expect the continued proliferation of alternative methods of care. As we will demonstrate later on in this chapter, many of these modalities are rich in cultural tradition and, for the purposes they serve, may be quite effective.

The continuing helix of increasing cost and diminishing accessibility for some will deepen the gap between those who are in direst need of health and mental health care and its availability. Those who are optimistic about the costs of health care delivery, especially to the poor, might realize that in this decade the reality of national health insurance has dimmed considerably and that governmental responsibility for the fiscal underwriting of health care continues to shrink as a matter of policy (usually in the guise of budget trimming and holding the line on inflation).[3]

Thus, it is conceivable that we will see a future in which both legitimate and questionable alternative health care systems, theories, and nostrums not only grow but, for many living on the economic margin, may become the only reasonable recourse. Perhaps physicians will realize that they are pricing themselves out of certain markets. Maybe they will understand how the high cost of health care erodes their prestige; maybe, but not likely. And as our system of health care erects sturdier barriers between itself and the poor and the culturally different, we can be sure that other systems of care will flourish; some of which may be harmful to users.

Drug use without medical supervision may be considered as part of the general growth of alternative health care means. It clearly is harmful. Other systems include diet and nutritional changes and supplements, physical fitness regimes, psychological approaches to physical healing, and various spiritually-based interventions, faith healing, for example. These may be harmful, entered into thoughtlessly, and may be the handiwork of charlatans, but they can be beneficial as well under proper conditions. For the poor and culturally different we may see a proliferation of folk medicine and culturally prescribed healing ministrations. Our ignorance and fear of such modes makes them difficult to evaluate, but it does seem obvious that most of them are integral parts of a cultural tradition and philosophy of healing, that, in itself, cannot be dismissed. Whatever the case, we are likely to see in the near future a continuing fragmentation in the delivery of health care — the consequences of which are, at this point, unknown.

When alternative health care modalities operate outside the purview of state and federal regulation, regulatory bodies, including the medical profession, attempt to bring them under regulation or prohibition, erring sometimes in the direction of overregulation. However, the growth of alternative systems of care for minorities of color is evidence that establishment health care is not doing its job effectively. The more widespread alternative health care practices become, the greater the need for substantial changes in conventional health care.

HEALTH AND MENTAL HEALTH CARE:
A CULTURAL CONTEXT

In our society not all people are equally healthy nor does everyone have equal access to the care that would facilitate good health. Some of the differences in the physical health of persons are related to natural events common to humankind: the disease process, aging, genetic predispositions, and expected biological transformations, for example. Other causes for differences in health, however, are related to cultural variations and sociopolitical inequalities that create barriers to access and utilization of health care resources. According to health utilization studies, usage (of services and facilities) is closely related to family income.[4,5,6] Striking differences are evident between lower- and higher-income groups in that the latter use health care services much more extensively.[7] Not only is there a significant relationship between income and use of health services, but there are other factors that influence accessibility and utilization. Some of those are political; some are cultural. What, then, are some of the specific cultural factors that create barriers to the utilization of health and mental health care services and cause some groups in our society to be less healthy and remain so.?[8]

Americans often seem reluctant to admit or understand that different cultural groups do differ in health status. Perhaps we sense it is impolitic to point to such differences, a violation of rules of civility and an implicit subversion of the ideology of democracy. For example we are acculturated not to notice when someone is physically disfigured, and the ordinary, informal rules of civil interaction (racist outbursts notwithstanding) seem to preclude making mention of or noticing another's ethnic background (particularly if it is an ethnic minority of color). These differences are significant, however, as we will demonstrate.

Fishman studied personnel of social service agencies in Atlanta, Georgia, in an attempt to ascertain their attitudes toward culture as a variable in service delivery. He found that the majority of those surveyed had little understanding of the importance and meaning of culture as a phenomenon in the provision of service. He asked those individuals who appeared to have some appreciation of culture as a factor how they thought that it affected the delivery of services. The key response was that culture was a sense of identification with a particular ethnic group, a presumed emotional and symbolic kinship with them.[9] The concept of *community* is important in the context of Fishman's study. People may actually belong to a particular ethnic community and dip from the same cultural well that other members of the community do, or they may share a symbolic or ideological tie with a group ethnically and racially different from them. Apparently such individuals are few in number — no less true in social service agencies than society at large. Generally, the idea of a grand social melting pot afflicts the majority of us when we think of our society and the groups making it up.

In terms of health and mental health care, two problems emerge. First, the health care system is a creation of the dominant culture and reflects the values, norms, patterns of interaction, etc., of that culture. Ethnically different groups sense that, and it may affect the likelihood of their utilizing health care services. Second, the differential patterns of utilization may lead directly to the differences in relative health of ethnic, racial, and class grouping in our society.

FACTORS IN HEALTH AND MENTAL HEALTH CARE UTILIZATION

Health can be defined as a state of complete physical, mental, and social well-being and not merely the absence of disease or infirmity. The enjoyment of the highest, attainable standard of health is one of the fundamental rights of every human being without distinction of race, religion, political belief, economics, or social condition. Thus, not only is health a state of wellness, but it is a right. In terms of the varying health of subgroups of our population, such a lofty notion is resonant in conception but weak in deed.

One reason for this, of course, is the differential access to and utilization of the health services that do exist. The availability and use of health care resources is a complex issue. The parameters of utilization are broad, ill-defined, and complicated by culture, geography, politics, social status, and the state of the economy. Offhand we can imagine various reasons for underuse of services: inadequate financial resources, geographical and social distance between would-be client and health service, and cultural conflicts between provider and recipient groups. Of course, other possibilities are more insidious: prejudice, institutional and individual racism, ignorance, and the maintenance of social power and status. (Some years ago, interns training in a large general hospital objected to their duty, especially in the emergency room, because they had to work with patients who were so different, culturally and socially, from them and who did not represent the populations they would be treating as full-fledged physicians.)

Geography

Health and mental health services may not be accessible to certain populations because of physical distance. The costs of transportation, the prospect of entering, perhaps, an alien social environment, the lack of child care services, and any number of factors exaggerate the problems of geographical inaccessibility.

The three major reasons for marked inequality in the distribution of health care resources (which in part, exaggerate the problems of inaccessibility and availability) include the following:

1. The basic ecological topography of society itself; various institutions appear to be aggregated in particular areas because of various demographic trends: population density, tax base, access to supporting institutions, and political supports.
2. Rural areas cannot attract and sustain an adequate resource base.
3. The segregation patterns of most metropolitan areas act as a barrier to easy and smooth access to many basic social resources for minorities.

Solutions to these problems, short of major upheavals in the demographic face of society, are often expensive, such as sending health care staff to satellite centers, and politically improbable.

Poverty

Poor people, when they are able, use the few resources available to them — general hospitals, emergency rooms, and inadequately staffed public clinics. They continually face the "difficulty of reaching a physician at night or on weekends, except through emergency rooms of local hospitals, long delays in obtaining appointments for routine care, and hurried and impersonal attention even after long hours wasted in waiting rooms."[10] In addition, some clinics operate Medicare and Medicaid mills, running as many people through as they possibly can, prescribing unnecessary treatment, and remaining inattentive to the needs of the individuals wanting service.

Another reason for underutilization of health services may be the views that some of the poor have developed about the human body and illness. In the opinion of Kosa, the poor are more likely to accept impaired bodily functioning as inevitable earlier and have greater tolerance for physical disability or malfunctioning and are sometimes indifferent to the ministrations of care-givers when they are incapacitated.[11]

To many of the poor, health care is a luxury higher up on their continuum of needs. Basic survival needs come first — food, shelter, a job — and other needs must await their relative satisfaction. Howard makes the observation that when she was planning a health care center in Mississippi, she had to be reminded that some people "saw as most relevant to their health, not medical care but the food, jobs, cash income, basic housing, shoes and clothing, clean water and the right to vote."[12]

Racism

To understand the nature of racism in health and mental health care delivery, we must distinguish between attitudes and actions. The term *prejudice* refers to the unfavorable feelings and attitudes that people harbor against others, especially other racial or ethnic groups. These are distinguished from unfavorable actions or behaviors, which fall under the heading of discrimination. For our purposes, however, the broader term *racism* conveys an impression of both prejudice and discrimination.

Racism in the health and mental health care system manifests itself in many, and often subtle, ways. For example the prejudiced and discriminatory manner in which many Anglo health care providers interact with minorities of color in emergency rooms and outpatient clinics in large public hospitals.[13] Weaver was correct when he said, ". . . the bureaucratic nature of clinics and emergency rooms with their insistence on forms and routine, in personal applications of procedures, on bending the clients to fit the organization, are major sources of complaints."[14]

It is obvious that minorities of color suffer from the practice of racism in the delivery of health and mental health care services. Many of them perceive such services as unresponsive to their needs, culturally insensitive, and, more importantly, racist.

Culture

The technology that the health and mental health system employs to achieve its desired outcomes must take into account the cultural differences of consumer clients. Failure to accommodate these differences may be perceived by some as suggesting the superiority of the dominant Anglo culture relative to other cultures. Krause, for example, refers to this failure as cultural chauvinism or cultural ethnocentrism.[15]

Providers in the health and mental health system, more so than in other service systems, need to be cognizant of the fact that all cultural groups have their own explanations of illnesses and strategies for curing illnesses and diseases. These explanations may be rational or irrational or rooted in historical experiences or in the spiritual cosmology of the particular culture. As a result, the health and mental health problems experienced by ethnic minorities of color cannot be completely understood within the framework of conventional Anglo-oriented theory and knowledge, for example dominant cultural conceptions of the causes, consequences, and treatment of health and mental problems.[16]

Conceptions of health and mental health problems and appropriate strategies of care are influenced by multiple elements of culture, for example religion and spirituality, psychosocial relations among group members, familial structural patterns, group composition, ascriptive and ascribed social roles, language, values and taboos, and beliefs and attitudes about health. Understanding the role these elements play in the seeking and utilization of formal health services is critical to assuring that these services are delivered in a culturally responsive and sensitive way.

Cultural groups vary in their responses to illness and pain, their perceptions of the severity and chronicity of various illnesses and diseases, their views regarding health and mental health professionals, and their folk beliefs regarding healing and curing. These differences influence, often in subtle ways, the attitudes and actions of members of particular cultures, and they interact with the health and mental health system.

Differences in Response to Illness and Pain

In an attempt to empirically assess the relationship between culture, illness, and pain, Zborowski studied differences in response to illness and pain by four ethnocultural groups, that is Jews, Italians, Irish, and "old Americans."[17] He found that, in general, Italians and Jews were more prone to exaggerate their illnesses and pain while the Irish tended to be stoical and able to bear a great deal of pain without complaining. Old Americans (those who Zborowski defined as native born, Protestant, and whose grandparents were born in the United States) tended to be the group most detached and unemotional in their responses. They did little complaining about illness and pain, were more apt to be able to accurately describe their symptoms, and were more likely to follow the advice and recommendations of the doctor relative to (procedures for cure) treatment. As a result, Old American-type patients were viewed by the medical profession as ideal patients. This characterization is important here because it is often in sharp contrast with the description given patients from minority groups who are frequently perceived as ignorant, uncooperative, unmotivated, and irresponsible when it comes to medical care, that is minority group patients are the hard to treat.

In a study similar to Zborowski's, five ethnocultural groups, that is Jews, Irish, Italians, Great Britains, and Germans, were examined regarding cultural differences in their health statuses and levels of health knowledge.[18] The groups were administered the Cornell Medical Index (designed to ascertain the respondent's level of knowledge of medical symptoms and his or her health status) to see if there were significant differences between them. The findings indicated that culture, as measured by ethnicity, was an important factor in perceptions and expressions of symptoms of illnesses and different cultures socialized their members to respond in different ways to illness and pain, for example the British are taught the "stiff upper lip," Italians and Jews have high affirmative responses to pain, while Germans, Irish, and Britains have low affirmative responses to illness and pain. These cultural differences become important when we consider how professionals vary in their tolerance for patients who exhibit differential responses to illness and pain.[19] It should be noted, however, that a wide variety of opinions about what constitutes an illness and pain exist among medical professionals. For some professionals "some conditions defined as illness in some settings are accepted as normal in others."[20]

Existing cultural literature indicates that there are important differences between groups in their perceptions and behaviors relative to the health and mental health system. It has been shown, for example, that "those individuals who belong to relatively more homogenous and cohesive cultural groups are more likely to react to illness and medical care in terms of the group's definition and interpretation of appropriate medical behavior rather than the more impersonalized prescriptions of the official medical care system."[21] Furthermore, those individuals who have culture-bound orientations toward illness and care are the ones most likely to delay seeking professional advice and treatment and, more importantly, they are the ones most likely to use home, folk, or cultural remedies when in need. Without a doubt, cultural predispositions relative to health and mental health (their causes, consequences, and cures) are important factors subverting and preventing the use of modern, scientifically respectable medical systems. Many Hispanics, for example, feel strongly alienated from the dominant culture and thus from health professionals who represent that culture.[22] They are leery about entering situations that perpetrate racial discrimination and cultural chauvinism. As a result they establish patterns of avoidance that lead them to underutilize formal health and mental health services, that is they seek these services only when everything else fails.[23]

Folk beliefs, religious beliefs, and orientations toward health and care sometimes are ambiguously related. It is difficult, if not impossible, to separate what a group considers religion or spiritual ritual and what it considers legitimate folk medicine. Most cultures have certain religious and spiritual practices that coincide with and are integral parts of the processes of healing and curing of physical and mental illnesses. Providers of formal services, therefore, must not only recognize these practices, more importantly they must make efforts to incorporate them into their helping technologies. Until this is done, we should not be surprised that the use rates for ethnic minorities of color will remain relatively low. If a particular cultural group believes that providers are sensitive to their cultural needs, they will be more inclined to use existing services. If, on the other hand, they sense that providers are culturally insensitive, they will seek alternative sources of care and their use rates will be low.

Differences in the Prevalence and Incidence of Physical and Mental Illness

It is difficult, if not impossible, to isolate those factors which are independently predictive of physical and mental health from those independently predictive of culture. They are, for all practical purposes, highly correlated. It is, however, probably true that cultural factors account for some of the variance in the incidence and prevalence of disease and illness among groups. Blacks, for example, have a higher incidence of hypertension than do most other racial and ethnic groups in our society. This may, in part, be explained in terms of differential genetic predispositions of the group relative to other groups, or it may just as well be related to cultural practices, such as the "soul" diet, orientation to physical exercise and exertion, and the understanding, acceptance, and use of medications as treatments measures. Whatever the case, genetic predispositions are usually dependent for manifestation, that is phenotype expression, on cultural practices. So, while there are both physical and genetic differences between groups in our society, it should be kept in mind that differences in illness and disease rates are probably best understood in terms of cultural heterogeneity. To illustrate, American Indians have noticeably higher rates of alcoholism than do other groups in our society.[24] On the one hand, this can be explained in terms of differential physiological sensitivity to the ethanol in alcohol. On the other hand, it can be explained by cultural phenomena and as concessions by Indians to the oppression of the dominant (Anglo) culture. We think both explanations are plausible.

Ethnic minorities of color have higher incidences of hypertension, diabetes mellitus, cardiovascular diseases, cancer, infectious diseases, fetal and neonatal mortality, etc., than do other ethnic groups in our society. Many of these problems, as we have suggested, are related to cultural characteristics of these groups. Others are related to environmental externalities associated with their lifestyles, living arrangements (living in slums, ghettos, and barrios), and living in dire poverty. Bracht clearly summarizes these issues in the following way:

> Those with less than $2,000 family income [a disporportionate number of whom are ethnic minorities of color — authors] report more than four times as many heart conditions as those in the highest income group, six times as much mental or nervous trouble; six times as much arthritis and rheumatism; six times as many cases of high blood pressure; over three times as many orthopedic impairments; and almost eight times as many visual impairments. The income level, less than $2,000, is heavily weighted for the aged, but the contrast at the next lowest level is still great, although not quite as dramatic.[25]

The point we are making is simply that living in poverty can make you sick; belonging to certain racial groups can give you a higher disposition to certain kinds of illnesses and diseases (both physical and mental); and being a member of a particular cultural group can involve you in situations that aggravate or lessen the likelihood and experience of being physically or mentally ill.

STRUCTURAL ELEMENTS IN THE HEALTH CARE SYSTEM: CULTURAL INSENSITIVITY

In the United States health care has a lustrous image (vocal critics notwithstanding), and the doctor stands as a prototype of what professionalism represents. In its evolution, the witchcraft of health and healing has submerged its magical religious origins and emerged as a complex system composed, in part, of complex technology, scientific precepts, and a doctrine that ". . . disease is avoidable . . . the only admissable evidence is objective . . . medical problems have medical solutions. . .and health professionals are the best providers for health needs."[26] Somewhere among these evolutionary paths, health care became detached from its humanistic tendencies, its compassionate concern for suffering, and its commitment to caring.

Today we have a manpower and facility-intensive medical system that is plagued with the problems of complex technology, excessive specialization of personnel, fragmented services, poor administration and management, and questionable costs relative to benefits. Within this system, however, there are professionals who still struggle to retain some of their humane origins, continue to remain advocates of humanity, and continue to push for systematic changes. But, fundamentally, the system has been resistive to minor, let alone major, changes. Health care providers (the basic wheels of the system), such as nursing homes, hospitals, home health agencies, health-maintenance organizations, and physicians, co-exist in mutual and sustaining relationships and run for the most part on business precepts and "free-market" ideology. The end result is a "protect-your-turf" syndrome that operates to perpetuate the problems of rising costs, inefficient management, maldistributions of resources and personnel, and inequalities of access.

Access to the System

One of the most important problems in medical care delivery is that of gaining access to the system by all segments of society. There is no question that Medicare and Medicaid have made medical care more available to the poor, medically indigent, aged, and some categories of the disabled. However, even within these programs there is differential treatment according to race, cultural backgrounds, and economic status.[27] Financial entitlement is only one aspect of the complex issue of access. Under current federal guidelines, access usually is available for states of morbidity, whereas health maintenance and preventive care is limited to more affluent segments of the population or through work-related health plans. Blacks, Hispanics, the poor, the working class, rural populations, and many of the elderly are virtually locked out of primary

care services. The maldistribution and ethnic imbalance of physicians in the community, transportation costs, and time required to
travel to medical care services are all closely correlated with utilization patterns.

The issue of access to health care services has been studied rather
consistently for the past ten years. Data from a national probability
sample of the American population reveals some interesting facts
about access to health services and utilization patterns of ethnic
minorities of color:

1. Minorities of color are much less likely than other groups to
   report having some form of health insurance coverage. The
   lack of coverage is significantly associated with low incomes
   and education.
2. Minority groups appear to use hospitals as much as the rest of
   the population but are somewhat less likely to have and use
   private physicians and dentists. The lack of health insurance
   coverage is related to the use of private physicians, and low
   education plays a significant role in the underutilization of
   dentists.
3. Minorities are generally more dissatisfied with the services
   they receive than are other segments of the population.
4. Minorities, in general, receive less care from physicians according to their needs than do other population groups.
5. Minorities are much more inclined to favor and use cultural
   and home remedies for certain types of illnesses than are other
   groups.[28]

These findings help us to appreciate some of the more important
reasons why minorities use the formal health care system less than
other segments of the population. As suggested, by the above study,
cultural characteristics, environmental and organizational constraints, and limited accessibility to the system influence utilization
patterns among minority groups.

As mentioned earlier, the major economic barrier to assessing the
health system has been eliminated for all practical purposes, for example with the implementation of the Medicaid and Medicare programs, financial barriers to receiving health care for ethnic
minorities, the poor and indigent, the aged, etc., have been removed. Since the health system is a subsystem of the larger political

and economic suprastructure of U.S. society, the conflicts that arise between corporate/bureaucratic and humanistic values can be expected to be projected into administrative and management decisions in health care. At the present time, health care is conceptually a right, but, pragmatically, it still remains a privilege in several areas of its management.

Despite a recognition that in the last decade there has been a shift in disease profiles from acute to chronic illness, health care continues to be predominantly organized around an acute medical model implying highly specialized interventions and time-limited hospitalization with the objective of cure. This is supported by the monitoring regulations and the rapid turnover of patient stay in hospitals. In chronic illnesses the focus is more on care and management over time, frequently accompanied by uncertain outcomes. In such conditions the primary objective is to attain the best quality of life possible for the patient as well as the family. Palliation and symptomatic relief must be readily available through consistency of care, most effectively delivered through a primary care model. For inner-city, ethnic-minority populations this is often sought through outpatient facilities or in hospital emergency rooms. There, patients are treated by a succession of physicians who respond to the immediate crisis but who are not tuned into paying attention to what they consider insignificant or who are unable to relate with sufficient knowledge to a patient's cultural background. Nonmedical (environmental, cultural, psychological, etc.) causes of illness, for example, can often be the basis for acute symptom manifestations. If the physician however, does not have the time nor the inclination to elicit in-depth information from the patient or to inform the patient about what is required of him or her, the episodes of illness keep repeating and the patient keeps returning for relief. A tragic example of failure to recognize a nonmedical causation is the extraordinary incidences of various forms of lead poisoning among poor children. The medical establishment, like the rest of us, has been slow to respond to this major threat to health.

For many ethnic minorities and poor people, the primary medical need is long-term care for chronic, more or less debilitating, conditions. It has been estimated that ". . . 50 percent of the population now suffers from chronic illnesses and these disorders account for 70 percent of all doctor visits."[29] Chronic illnesses, such as emphysema, hypertension, kidney disease, and diabetes, require active involvement and responsibility of the patient in maintaining optimal functioning. Patients need to be given updated information on a periodic basis about the course of their illnesses. They must be taught appropriate ways to maintain their physical stability and when to respond to perceived crises by seeking professional help. This approach implies a consumer-centered model of health and medical care. It also implies a recognition on the part of the providers that self-help groups and family and community networks must be permitted to enter into the diagnostic and treatment spheres and that the curing mandate cannot be lodged totally with the physician or other allied health professionals. As Gartner and Riessman state, "The mutual aid concept, of course, also includes the role of the group and the 'helper-therapy' dimension. Both self-care and mutual aid activities are movements away from 'medio-centrism' and emphasize the power and responsibility individuals have for their own well-being."[30] All too frequently, however, providers offer medication to their patients as a substitute for listening and responding in a sensitive and humane way.

There is still another important issue that needs to be addressed. Although medical care technology and scientific medical research have helped people live longer and therefore made them candidates for chronic illnesses, the stressful components of living, nutritional deficits, and unhealthy environments have also contributed to chronicity. The crucial question is, can the organization of health delivery via its current bureaucratic model be infused with more of a public health orientation of illness prevention and health promotion? The increase in chronic illness and disease is particularly dramatic among ethnic minority groups. This creates excessive demands upon the existing medical care system to treat these illnesses at the expense of others. There seem to be no major efforts to link needs, demand, and supply into a functionally sound and cost-effective model of health care, which is capable of addressing primary, secondary, and tertiary levels of need. In the present system, unfortunately, the major providers of help, physicians, create their own demands, practicing where and to some extent on whom they please. As a result, ethnic minorities of color receive more than their fair share of ineffective, poor quality, and culturally insensitive health and medical care.

THE NEED FOR CULTURALLY SENSITIVE PRIMARY CARE

Failure to have a personal physician for a large segment of the population, namely the ethnic minorities, has led them into the impersonal, fragmented ambulatory care system of institutional medicine. They often delay seeking help, if they seek it at all, until symptoms become severe and serious. Many stress-related symptoms are being treated at high cost in these institutions, with elaborate, excessive, and unnecessary technology.

Culturally sensitive primary care can offer inner-city and rural populations the advantages of easier access, health maintenance, prevention of disability through early detection, referral for specialized care, and continuity with the same physician. This is a more humanistic type of care based upon better physician understanding of the whole person and his or her life-style.

Until recently concern about inequities in the delivery of primary care services came primarily from groups that were ". . . underprivileged because of race, poverty or geographic location," but went unheeded because such groups had less "status, money, and political power."[31] Now, the revitalization of the primary care movement emanates from those in power who are finding the system excessively costly and dysfunctional, too.

In most of the intragroup ethnic-alternative approaches to health care, the processes of translating signs of sickness into symptoms, and ultimately into the naming of an illness, are culturally prescribed. At whatever level of specialization nonphysician healers (herbalists, curanderos, medicine men, spiritists, root doctors, witch doctors, etc.) in Hispanic, black, and native American communities share the beliefs, values, symbolisms, and languages of the groups that they help, and there is no marked cultural hiatus. In addition, the objectives of curing and healing are fundamentally social and spiritual and, as a result, accountability for illness and sickness is seen as deriving from natural causes, witchcraft, and dead ancestors. All of these causal conditions are mutually understood and accepted by the patient group as well as the healer.

Once the individual in need enters the formal medical care system, the family, extended kin network, and friendship support systems cease being directly involved in the curing processes. Formalized medical care adopts a patient-physician model of treatment and cure, rather than a patient-group-physician or social model. If the family or other support groups are considered at all they are usually assigned to allied health personnel, namely social workers, who act as conduits to the wider patient world.

The doctor-patient relationship is an interpersonal communication system that relies upon a flow of information, ideas, and emotions, both verbal and nonverbal. Imparting of information that is fundamental to medical compliance can become highly problematic when there is cognitive/emotional incompatibility between the receiver and the transmitter, when there are unstated assumptions that create ambiguities, when the flow of messages are blocked because of high anxiety in the patient, when authoritative control is exercised by the physician and the patient or family is not encouraged to respond, or when the physician simply does not listen or acts with indifference. A physician socialized with middle-class standards and who has no particular awareness of ethnic differences will probably not be too successful in sustaining the therapeutic medical alliance.

Edward Spicer has stated that "in complex societies like our own, there is never a single homogenous tradition guiding the medical arts. At least as many healing traditions exist as there are peoples with different ethnic backgrounds."[32] The trained physician is taught to believe that scientific medicine is the only thing that works, but the patient's environments, which he must enter, have many medical traditions, beliefs, and practices of their own. Health care systems are both social and cultural systems, "They are not simply systems of meanings and behavioral norms, but those meanings and norms are attached to particular social relationships and institutional settings."[33] Thus, ethnic medical care traditions contain differing concepts of body and mind, differing perceptions of illness, health and sick-role behavior, differing types of healers, and different processes of healing. All of these aspects of the system are interrelated and governed by socially sanctioned rules. In essence, any ethnic health tradition is deeply encoded in the identity of the particular group.

Ethnic medical systems have well-defined popular, folk, and professional sectors that are not tightly class-bound but are practiced to varying degrees by all members of the group. Kleinman states that these sectors are separate constructs that organize health beliefs, behaviors, and caring relationships. He refers to them as culturally determined clinical realities that underpin a system of cultural healing. Each one of these sectors explains illness, health, causality, and cure in different ways. Kleinman refers to these as explanatory models that are culture-specific.[34]

Hispanic Americans

Hispanic populations are heterogenous, coming from different countries and socioeconomic classes. It is expected that this population will rapidly increase to 55.3 million in the U.S. in the year 2000, the median age will be 20.7 years, and there will be twice as many children under five years than the rest of the population.[35] Despite their origin, a number of health traditions are commonly practiced by all Hispanic Americans.

A strong tradition in the Hispanic culture is that of herbal medicine. This tradition has fully developed pharmacopeia, culturally defined rituals for preparing herbal mixtures, and legitimized folk healers (herbalists) and pharmacies (botanicas) where the herbs are sold. Puerto Ricans turn to this type of treatment for cure of both "natural" and "unnatural" illnesses.[36] Herbal remedies are taken in conjunction with medications prescribed by modern medicine and conceivably can create problems since some of these are fairly potent and have specific effects on the body.

There is another folk tradition for classifying diseases, foods, and medicines along a hot-cool-cold continuum, which is based on humoral theory. This is consistent with a concept of balance and imbalance that characterizes health and disease.[37] A cold disease requires hot foods and hot medications. There is great local and idiosyncratic variation in these classifications. Professionals who prescribe for Hispanic people need to question them closely about these personal beliefs, particularly in pediatric care. A study of a Puerto Rican neighborhood in New York City revealed some problems with this folk tradition in an outpatient pediatric department of a large hospital. In infant feeding, the usual evaporated milk formula is considered hot and whole milk considered cold. When these infants develop rashes that were considered to be hot, the mothers precipitously switched the infants to whole milk (cold), or else the introduced neutralizing or cool substances, such as magnesium carbonate, barley water, or mannitol. Both practices resulted in the infants' developing diarrhea.[38] This kind of symbolic duality is also found in other cultures, such as the Chinese, where foods are classified according to a Yin-Yang tradition.

The belief in espiritismo is deeply ingrained in Hispanic cultures. Spiritist doctrine accepts a dichotomy between material forms and spirits. The former is destructible; the latter is indestructible and can work for good or evil. Diagnosis and cure of medical and social problems are effected through a faith healer (medium or spiritist) by means of communication with the spirit world. Manifestations of auditory hallucinations, spirit possession, and trances are accepted healing processes. Hispanics go to mediums when they have problems stemming from "unnatural" sources. It is a type of crisis intervention through which they are reintegrated into the social life of the group. The ceremony takes place at *centros* which are familiar, comfortable community organizations. There is no negative labeling, only a process of defining the cause in external spirit terms. Treatment is carried on within a group supportive context. Fees are charged according to what the person can afford to pay, and the symbols of healing are familiar. "Like many social institutions, it is multifunctional, contributing to the social and psychological well-being of its adherents by serving as a voluntary organization, a way of ordering social relationships; a religion, and an identity."[39]

An awareness of a belief in spiritism is extremely important in working Puerto Rican patients. All too frequently behaviors are labeled inappropriate or pathological when they are expressions in a different construction of reality and are internally consistent with a belief system not familiar or acceptable to the Western-trained health professional.

The ethnomedical system of Mexican-American people, in addition to the herbal and food traditions, includes a category referred to as "Mexican disease . . . illness that the Anglo doctor does not recognize." This category is fairly well-defined, containing such classifications as magical fright (*mal de susto*), fallen fontanel (*mollera caida*), cachexia (*latido*), indigestion infection (*empacho*), and grunting *pujo*).[40] Each one of these has its own prescriptions for treating, although it is claimed that regional modifications have been noted. There are also definite ethnomedical rules, with local variations, governing fertility, childbearing, and child-rearing, that need to be understood by Western providers of health care. The suggestion is offered that Spanish patients be questioned carefully about what help they have already sought for their symptoms when they present themselves to the physician and that some attempt be made to understand their perception of their symptoms so that treatment can be structured within a cultural frame of reference. Over and over again it has been demonstrated that whenever it is economically possible, Hispanic people use formal medical care services in conjunction with their own ethnomedical systems.

In Hispanic families where the male role is more rigidly defined (machismo) the involvement of the husband/father becomes an issue to be considered carefully before any medical decision is made with respect to the family. The feminine role definition is changing in Hispanic families as well as in the rest of the U.S. In such a time of transition, providers of medical care need to be particularly cognizant of these factors in helping Hispanic patients make decisions. There are a number of other cultural values that are part of the world view of Hispanic people, such as the importance of privacy, the attitude of respect, the importance of the personal relationship, and the reliance on immediate and extended family, which govern their behavior as they interact with the modern health care system.

Black Americans

Black Americans are also a heterogenous people coming from different origins and socioeconomic classes. In similar fashion to Hispanic people, black Americans have some basic popular and folk medical traditions. Some of these have evolved historically from plantation practices, a number of which have African roots. Causes of illness, for example, are classified into three categories: natural, occult, and spiritual. Witchcraft, hexing, root work, voodoo, and reading of signs are used in occult curing. Spiritual curing needs the intervention of God. "Through the laying on of hands, through prayer, through the use of prayer cloths, and through various exercises of faith, a person is made well."[41] In this way a person achieves "renewal" and sins are dissolved.

There is a tendency among some black people to lump together all kinds of illnesses and not to seek to identify a particular one.

When one falls ill, one refers to having "the misery."[42] There is often a blend of the three illness categories, and persons go to different types of healers simultaneously. Black populations who migrate from southern rural areas to northern cities bring these traditions with them and persist in using them together with formal medical care services.

A dietary health-related behavior that remains fairly well entrenched in some black women is the practice of eating starch. This has caused obesity and iron-deficiency anemia. It is claimed that in some localities as many as 40 percent of pregnant women eat packaged laundry starch. It sometimes begins at pregnancy and continues thereafter. It is eaten secretively and not told to the physician. The precise reason for this is not known. There are a number of beliefs associated with this practice, but it may also be genetic. There seems to be some evidence that women who do this have children who later eat plaster. Providers of medical care need to be alert to this possibility.

Social and emotional stresses in the lives of many black Americans have led to a high degree of somatization and to such conditions as elevated blood pressure levels, and later, hypertensive heart disease and stroke. Hypertension is a major health problem today. It is estimated that 20 percent of people under forty-five suffer from some illness connected with these. Black people make up 19 percent of the known hypertensive cases but comprise only 11 percent of the total U.S. population. Although heredity, sex, and place of residence correlate with the elevation of blood pressure, a dissonance between the social milieu in later life and expectations based on early experiences during the individual's developmental stages may also be critical correlates. We, among others, suspect that these correlates, in part, are instrumental is setting in motion the individual's biological defense mechanisms, which, in turn, upsets the person's organismic homeostasis and leads to a significant elevation of systolic arterial blood pressure.[43]

Native Americans

The cultural health care practices of native Americans resemble those of other ethnic minority cultures in many ways. There are, however, some significant behavioral differences, and certain values underlying these practices are unique to them: harmony between man and nature, that is nature in the native American view of the world, is one thing and a person is only part of that one thing; one accepts the world and does not try to change it; man has the innate ability to control supernatural forces; and there is the belief in death and rebirth. Such values manifest themselves in the processes of symbolic healing, which has been characterized by some as ". . . suggestion, persuasion, or placebo effects."[44]

Because of the extensive tribal variations among native American groups, any discussion of their health and mental health practices must focus on specific tribal approaches to healing and curing. Each tribal entity and nation has its own culture, economic system, and education and welfare system. Moreover, each entity has a health care system comprised of medicine people (men and women), apprentices, and helpers, each having specific and limited abilities, responsibilities, and rights. As a result healing rituals and ceremonies involve many members of the local tribal community.

Native Americans, in general, value strong identification with their families of origin and extended families. These family systems are not only related to each other but are also related to other clans and tribal systems and serve as the major source of mutual support, sustenance, and cultural identity for its members. Family systems are actively involved in the healing and curing of family members in need.

If health services for native Americans are to be culturally sensitive, they must be delivered in ways that recognize their history, strengths, and culture. Local tribal health care systems exist (specific rituals and ceremonies, as pointed out, vary from tribe to tribe) and are providing positive services. Professional providers must recognize these and involve them in the service delivery process.

CHANGING THE SYSTEM: A CULTURAL FRAMEWORK

Given the grim reality of the health and mental health statuses of ethnic minority populations, it is quite imperative that innovative and alternative strategies for health care delivery be sought. Many community-targeted approaches have been tried in the past and some are currently in operation, that is neighborhood, indigenous health aides and paraprofessionals, outreach programs, walk-in clinics, crisis centers, hot lines, etc. These efforts, often times fragmented and uncoordinated, have never been unified programmatically nor infused with a holistic philosophy of care. As a result, the system has been unaware, insensitive, and unresponsive to the cultural needs of ethnic minorities. Changing the system, however, appears to be an overwhelming task. The high cost of medical care, the differences in what it means to be healthy or sick for various population groups, and the differences in the treatment received by various groups makes the notion of systemic change complex.

Mechanic was cautious in relating public expectations to health care changes when he stated, "Whatever our aspirations might be, there are no indications that in the near future we will experience a radical transformation in our values, or economic system [or health system — authors], or in the distribution of wealth."[45] It is one thing to be aware and understand that people differ physically, psychologically, and culturally in significant ways and quite another to undo the human tendency to espouse one's values and culture above another and to be willing to share one's personal resources with one another.

There has been some confusion in the health literature as to what systemic changes are needed to improve the current delivery structure. In an attempt to deal appropriately with changes needed in the system, Howard, on the other hand, concluded that it is important for practitioners to recognize the inherent worth, uniqueness, and wholeness of patients and, more importantly, decision-making responsibilities relative to care should be shared between patients and practitioners.[46] Kosa and Zola, on the other hand, concluded that structural changes in the delivery system are most necessary, for example developing innovative financing arrangements; special incentives for health care institutions and organizations to innovate; evolving specialized health, therapeutic, and educational programs for those in need; and developing innovative human relations training programs for practitioners.[47] Bracht, in attempting to isolate other areas in need of change, indicated that the most troubling aspect of the current system is the growing overdependence of the population on services. He noted, "The single most important corrective action required to reduce excessive demand for health care is in the appropriate education of the American public regarding the use of medical treatment. Extensive effort must be made to educate people regarding which symptoms need attention by physicians or nurse practitioners. Ways in which individuals can assume increasing responsibility for their own health maintenance must be accelerated."[48]

All of these suggestions are probably relevant to improving the current system. As far as we are concerned, however, they are superficial and cosmetic approaches to the problem. What is really needed are major substantive changes. We suggest that the single most important change required is for decision makers to develop and institutionalize culturally sensitive modalities of holistic health care. Perhaps these approaches coupled with current approaches (those that are rational, scientifically-oriented, and highly technological) can have some real value in the treatment and cure of ethnic minorities of color. It seems to us that it would be wholly inappropriate to disregard the cultural health care practices of ethnic minority groups. Rather, systematic efforts should be made to incorporate these into current and future models of care.

We have indicated thoroughout this chapter (both explicitly and implicitly) that health professionals who have been selected, trained, and certified by the standards of the dominant culture are not prepared to deal with individuals who come from different racial and/or cultural groups whose values, attitudes, and general lifestyles are different from their own. It seems to us that these professionals are more interested in the goal of serving the psychological needs of the Caucasian middle class, to which a vast majority of them belong, rather than effectively meeting the needs of persons from culturally diverse backgrounds. This reinforces our belief that those responsible for formulating health policies, designing health programs, implementing these programs, and training service delivery personnel must, without any doubt, consider the physical, psychological, and cultural predispositions of target populations if services are to be effective in meeting needs. This consideration is an important first step in the development of culturally relevant programs and services. Moreover, we feel strongly that cultural sensitivity must be the underlying principle of contemporary and future systemic change, change that will assure the enjoyment of the highest attainable standard of health (physical and mental) for all.

REFERENCES

1. Bracht, Neil F.: *Social Work in Health Care: A Guide to Professional Practice.* New York, The Haworth Press, 1978.
2. Waterhouse, Alan: The advent of localism in two planning cultures. *Town Planning Review, 50*:322, July 1979.
3. *National Health Insurance.* Hearing before the Subcommittee on Health of the Committee on Ways and Means, House of Representatives, 96th Congress, 2nd Session, February 11, 12, and 21, 1980, Vol. 2, Serial 96-91. U.S. Government Printing Office, Washington, D.C., 1980.
4. *Health Status of Minorities and Low-Income Groups,* U.S. DHEW, HRA, OHRO, No. (HRA 79-627). Washington, D.C., 1979.
5. *Health of the Disadvantaged — Chart Book II,* USDHEW, HRA, OHRA, No. (HRA 80-633). Washington, D.C., 1980.
6. *Use of Health and Mental Health Outpatient Services in Four Organized Health Care Settings,* USDHEW, PHS, NIMH, No. 1. Rockville, MD., 1980.
7. Krause, Elliot A.: *Power and Illness.* New York, Elxevier, North-Holland, Inc., 1977.
8. Kane, Robert L., Kasteler, Josephine, and Gray, Robert M.: *The Health Gap.* New York, Springer Publishing Co., 1976.
9. Fishman, Robert J.H.: A note on culture as a variable in providing human services in social service agencies. *Human Organization, 38(2)*:189-196, 1979.
10. Kosa, John, and Zola, Irving, K.: *Poverty and Health.* Cambridge, Harvard University Press, p. 299.
11. *Ibid.*
12. Howard, Jan, and Strauss, Anselm: *Humanizing Health Care.* New York, Wiley-Interscience Publication, 1975.
13. Hammond, Karl E.: Blacks and the urban health crisis. *Journal of the National Medical Association,* pp. 226-231, May 1974.
14. Weaver, Jerry: *National Health Policy and the Underserved.* St. Louis, C.V. Mosby Co., 1976, p. 23.
15. Krause, *op. cit.*
16. Clark, Margaret: *Health in the Mexican-American Culture.* Los Angeles, University of California Press, 1959.
17. Zborowski, Mark: Cultural components in response to pain. *Journal of Social Issues, 8*:16-30, 1952.
18. Coog, Sydney: Ethnic origins, educational level and responses to a health questionnaire. *Human Organization, 20:*65-69, 1961.
19. *Ibid.*
20. Kane, Kasteler, and Gray, *op. cit.*
21. Editorial: Social patterns of illness and medical care. *Journal of Health and Human Behavior, 6*:6-16, 1965.
22. Kane, Kasteler, and Gray, *op. cit.*
23. *Ibid.*
24. Waddel, Jack O., and Everett, Michael N.: *Drinking Behavior Among Southwestern*

Indians: An Anthropological Perspective. Tucson, The University of Arizona Press, 1980.

25. Bracht, *op. cit.,* p. 104.

26. Boyce, T., and Michael, M.: Assumptions of western man. *Man and Medicine, 1(4)*:311, Summer 1976.

27. Anderson, Ronald, et al. *Access to Medical Care Among the Latino Population.* Unpublished paper presented at the American Public Health Association Meeting, Los Angeles, California, October 1978.

28. *Ibid.*

29. Gartner, Alan, and Riessman, Frank: *Self-Help in the Human Services.* New York, Jossey-Bass, 1977.

30. *Ibid.* p. 91.

31. Rogers, David E. The challenge of primary care. In Knowles, John H. (Ed.): *Doing Better and Feeling Worse.* New York, W.W. Norton and Company, 1977, p. 58.

32. Spicer, Edward H.: *Ethnic Medicine in the Southwest.* Tucson, University of Arizona Press, 1977.

33. *Ibid.,* pp. 7-8.

34. Kleinman, Arthur: Concepts and a model for the comparison of medical systems as cultural systems. *Social Science and Medicine, 12(2B)*:85, April 1978.

35. *Ibid.,* pp. 86-87.

36. *Task Panel Reports.* Submitted to the President's Commission of Mental Health, Vol. III, Appendix, February 1978.

37. Delgado, Melvin: Herbal medicine in the Puerto Rican community. *Health and Social Work, 4(2),* May 1979.

38. Currier, Richard L.: The hot-cold syndrome and symbolic balance in Mexican and Spanish-American folk medicine. *Ethnology, 5*:251-263, July 1966.

39. Harwood, Alan: The hot-cold theory of disease. *Journal of the American Medical Association, 216*:1153-1158, May 15, 1971.

40. Kay, Margarita A.: Health and illness in a Mexican-American barrio. In Spicer, Edward H. (Ed.): *Ethnic Medicine in the Southwest.* Tucson, University of Arizona Press, 1977, pp. 99-166.

41. Mitchell, Faith: *Voodoo Medicine.* New York, Cannon and Johnson Co., 1978, pp. 19-166.

42. Spicer, *op. cit.,* pp. 7-8.

43. Cassel, Henry: Psychosocial factors in essential hypertension. *American Journal of Epidemiology, 90(3)*:171-200, 1969.

44. Sanders, Donald F.: Navaho medicine. *Human Nature,* July 1978, pp. 54-62.

45. Mechanic, David: *Public Expectations and Health Care.* New York, Wiley Interscience Publication, 1972, p. 84.

46. Howard and Strauss, *op. cit.,* pp. 139-140.

47. Kosa and Zola, *op. cit.*

48. Bracht, *op. cit.,* p. 44.

Chapter 5

A TRANSCULTURAL PERSPECTIVE
ON FAMILY AND CHILDREN'S SERVICES

I N America it is often thought, thanks perhaps to the cumulative influence of Robert Young, Ozzie and Harriet, the Cleavers, the Brady Bunch and other electronic families, that the standard family has mother and father, two to four children, all living under the same roof and that father works to bring home the bacon (or, rather, steak) and mom stays at home and keeps kith, kin, and kitchen together and, although subordinate to the authority of her spouse, is significant for the provision of nurturant glue. The kids are basically decent, although they run a continual gamut of hormonal explosions and interpersonal troubles, which bring a knowing twinkle to their parents' eyes. Unconsciously or not and whether or not these mythic families reflect a desire or create it, we may measure our own families against these implicit ideals and, falling short or coming up deviant, we may feel vaguely uncomfortable or downright ashamed.

The fact is, however, in spite of this glimmering electronic and moral image, less than 10 percent of the families in this country conform to it.[1] In most American families both parents work, one parent raises the children, mother but not father works, aunts or uncles or grandparents assume most of the responsibility for child-rearing, or children are raised in homes or settings other than that of the biological parents. Our prevailing culture imagery of the family, although not very accurate, is not just a piece of beguiling froth. It is a view, sturdy in its persistence, that colors the social policies and programs supporting and serving the families and children of this nation. In addition, the image shapes our collective judgments about those families who depart markedly from it. Such cultural imagery blinds us to the enormous variety of family structures and life-styles and renders the view of family (which support policy and practice) perilously and perniciously narrow. A classic consequence of such thinking is the much heralded (and amply hooted) *Moynihan Report.* Criticized on a number of grounds from inherent bias and racism to methodological quirks, the report (*The Negro Family: The Case for Na-*

tional Action), as we interpret it, had a basic flaw: it was blissfully wed to the dominant cultural view of the family.[2] The alarm expressed in the report at the number of black families without male heads and the subsequent plunge into speculation about that fact and the presumed consequence of widespread personal and social disorganization within the black community overlooked —

1. the reality that the majority of black families, even those mired in their third or fourth generation of poverty, were intact by the report's own standards
2. the critical importance (in terms of survival, socialization, and cultural integrity) of the extended family
3. the vitality and energy of the core black culture
4. the fact that the so-called destruction of the breadwinner role for many black families was not basically a cultural fact but, instead, a social and political fact requiring alterations in the institutions and policies that surround and support family life.[3]

In this chapter we will briefly outline and review some of the policies and services affecting families and children in this country, examine the ideologies and assumptions fueling the policies, suggest some "truths" or corrective ideas about minority families (black and Hispanic, primarily), analyze the organizational context of service delivery as a cultural phenomenon, one with the potential to subvert effective service, and suggest pathways for change in the direction of truly transcultural service.

POLICIES AND SERVICES FOR FAMILIES AND CHILDREN: BASIC ASSUMPTIONS

Alfred Kadushin makes the most useful distinctions between kinds of family and child welfare services: supportive, designed to help families maintain their integrity during times of inordinate stress and conflict; supplementary, designed to complement parental roles when deficiencies there seriously threaten the parent/child role system; and substitutive, wherein the damage to the parent/child relationship is so widespread that a temporary or permanent dissolution of the relationship is required and the child must move into another role system.[4] We will use these definitions as a heuristic guide through our hurried tour of child and family welfare services.

The United States has no generic family policy, one created to underwrite and support each and every family in this country. Perhaps the closest we come is *Aid to Families with Dependent Children (AFDC)*. We have already discussed AFDC as an income maintenance program and the philosophy supporting income transfer and redistributive policy. In this chapter, we want to examine it as a policy (and complex of services) supporting family life. If it is the case that AFDC is our basic family policy, all the more is regrettable, since the impact of the program has been to divide as many families as are saved.[5]

AFDC is a supplementary program, its most benign assumption being that economic assistance will flesh out the parental role sufficiently well that the parent/child system can remain intact. Noble sentiment aside, when most of us think of welfare and welfare abuse, the rip-offs and cons, and the spectacular boondoggles of ingenious clients, we are thinking of AFDC. While the community may think that AFDC is a lucrative way for families to survive without work, the point of the program is to provide support for children in situations where mother cannot work, father is absent, and the children need support. To receive benefits a woman must, as best she can, remove any clue that she may be consorting with a male (the presumption being that he is providing financial support) and, with few exceptions and considerable variability between the states, benefits do not elevate one from penury, and the patchwork of accompanying social services for such families is uneven, if not unraveling and, in some cases, positively threadbare.

The reigning philosophy of AFDC is that financial and in-kind benefits provided should never be more than the sparest wage paid in the job market. Benefits, in other words, should never be seen as a substitute for money earned at work and they should be determined by a utilitarian calculus; benefits should be only sufficient enough to meet the barest need and deficient enough to act as a spur to employment. The strident emphasis on the value of work and the continuing devaluation of welfare are boosted by the belief that work is available for those who want it. This, in spite of the fact that —

1. As a society we maintain — as a matter of inflation-fighting policy — a fluctuating but sizeable population of unemployed.
2. Many, if not most, of the women receiving benefits do not have many "marketable" skills.

3. Should they find work these mothers then confront inadequate day-care services for their children, expensive outlays for transportation, clothes, and incidental expenses.
4. Available jobs pay poorly, and given the expenses of going to work, employment is a costly proposition.

Another dimension of the philosophy is that the benefits provided through AFDC are not an entitlement but rather a collective gratuity funneled through various governmental channels (charity as opposed to justice).[5] These assumptions and ideas present an imposing barrier to the consideration and development of a national policy for families and children (such as family or childrens' allowances, basic minimum income, a national system of day care, health insurance, and adequate public housing, programs provided in varying extent in most of the Western world).

Underlying the niggardliness of AFDC (in no state, even the most generous, does the AFDC payment provide a family income equal to the officially defined level of need)[6] lurks the prevalent cultural standard of family life discussed previously. Because these families are perceived as deviant, they are treated so. The attitudes toward them are often the same that we might expect toward the flagrant flouter of social decency and civil order. Rather than fostering the socialization of these families we apply social control measures, both formal and informal, to them. The painful irony is, of course, that any efforts to become "respectable" families are immediately discouraged by a combination of meagre, begrudged benefits, and deleterious attitudes.

More black and Hispanic families and children, by percentage, suffer from poverty than other groups, with the exception of native Americans. In 1974, 42 percent of all black children lived in poverty, nearly 22 percent of all Hispanic children, compared to 13 percent of white children.[7] In that same year 46 percent of the children receiving AFDC benefits were black, 47 percent were white, and Hispanic children made up about 14 percent of the white group.[8] Yet the 8 million children who are on the AFDC rolls are only slightly less than half of all children who live in official poverty (a definition some think is far too low). The proposals of the Reagan administration that pertain to AFDC will, over the long haul, more than likely reduce the number of people covered by the program but have no effect on the total number of families living in poverty.[9] So, many black and Hispanic families will face another threat to the basic building block of family life: secure income.

Even if benefits were adequate, families supported by AFDC take their help in an atmosphere of suspicion, prejudice, and humiliation. Public notions about welfare recipients are so negative and distorted that thousands of families who are probably eligible for benefits do not seek them.[10] Some of the more blatant misconceptions that families on AFDC hold follow:

The parents of recipients (the children) are able-bodied adults content to suck the charitable vein of the community dry. The fact is that most AFDC families are headed by a single mother raising young children — a female who, more than likely, has very few skills the job market demands. About 5 percent of the AFDC families receive benefits in the unemployed parent (AFDC-UP) segment of the program. Twenty-six states have opted for this program, which permits two-parent families to be eligible for benefits if the father is unemployed and can meet strict conditions pertaining to job training and the seeking and accepting of work.[11]

AFDC promotes illegitimacy and explosive birth rates. In truth, most illegitimate children are *not* on AFDC and most children on AFDC are *not* illegitimate.

Living off welfare is tantamount to living on Easy Street. As we have pointed out, in no state do AFDC benefits lift the recipient family to the official poverty line.

Parents of recipient children should be rehabilitated and trained for work. Even if jobs were available, training, which is continually cut, is for only a few. People working on the lower end of the economic scale do not welcome the idea of more people competing for their jobs at, perhaps, a lower salary. And the support required to nourish job training, job finding, and continued employment is simply not there, nor have most communities shown much of an inclination to provide it. Expecting people to work under conditions that seriously mitigate against it only adds pressure, not promise, for these families.[12]

In sum, the major program designed to support and sustain family life under deprived economic conditions, conditions extensive in their effect on black and Hispanic families, is insufficient to meet the needs of these families. Furthermore it is nourished on public hostility, misconception or, in good times, indifference. Both the process and the context in which benefits and services are administered have the effect of subverting self-esteem, family pride, and family continuity. The costs of the subsequent failures of AFDC (chronic unemployment, incomplete education, crime, ill health) are enormous in dollars, but the human costs are staggering. Lack of genuinely humane attention to this program (at the policy level) continues to cause human and social suffering. The cumulative personal and family tragedies that result from our failure to shore up and sustain family life are hardly worth the gain realized by cutting back and down on benefits and services.

Beyond AFDC, the largest service for black and Hispanic families, lies a network of family services, which in Kadushin's classification are supportive. These services are the "first line of defense" of the family threatened by internal and external stressors and provide an array of accommodations and supports from family therapy to family life education. Many of these agencies operate under the aegis of the Family Service Association of America (FSAA). In 1975, the member agencies saw 500,000 families and about 2,000,000 individuals.[13] While FSAA member agencies total 300, another 700 agencies exist, many of them under sectarian auspice,[14] that perform similar functions. Finally, there are about 200 children guidance clinics, and in 1976 they saw almost 300,000 children, though less than one-half that number received treatment.[15] For some time these agencies have been criticized for not attracting more minority clientele. The National Association of Black Social Workers, for example, has been especially vocal in this regard. A study completed in 1973 revealed that 20 percent of the clientele of member FSAA agencies were black, but this percentage had dropped from 23 percent in 1960.[16] However, other minority groups were seriously underrepresented in the case loads of these agencies. The agencies themselves have continued to call for organizational and intervention strategies designed to increase minority participation in their programs, but as yet, much remains to be accomplished.

Family and child guidance services are obviously a potentially valuable resource for minority families, families often subject to persistent and intense social and economic stressors. The underutilization of these resources by minority groups has many causes no doubt, but two complexes of factors may be particularly important: aspects of the organizational provision of services and assumptions of the professional model of service. The building of organizations providing therapeutic services tends to be around the clinical/consulting room model. Three assumptions of this model tend to stultify the possibility of transcultural development:

1. The theories and technical operations of therapy have evolved from a white, middle-class sociohistorical context, presume a rationalized bureaucratic structure for their delivery, and are, most likely, culture-bound.

2. Models and theories of intervention discount or dilute the importance of social structure and culture in the creation of and adaptation to human misery.

3. Because the organization of these services is based on a clinical bureaucratic model certain requirements of and assumptions about clients are typically made:

   a. The client must seek out the service and come to the agency.

   b. Fees (however minimal) for service must be rendered.

   c. Clients must be highly motivated.

   d. The focus of concern is the individual (sometimes the family).

   e. The community is of little importance in either the creation of the problem or the provision of social resources to combat the problem.

   f. There is a problem and, like a physical lesion, it can be excised by the deft use of the counselor's tools.[17]

Possibly the most hardy of these barriers in the organization of the clinic is the intrapsychic model of counseling. Not only does it presume certain structural requisites (individual and enclosed rooms and offices and structured social distance between client and helper, for instance), it also encourages the interpretation of culturally inspired expressions and behaviors as merely psychological. For example the inferred indolence (perhaps thought to equal a sign of depression or neurasthenic withdrawal) of Indian parents in dealing with their son's problem at school may be, instead, an example of the prized trait of durable patience. The seeming diffidence of the father when confronted by the worker about the problem may be the Indian's unwillingness to stare into a stranger's face and challenge his view; to do so would be to be rude and lack grace.[18] In another hypothetical instance the family service worker might be horrified to learn that her black client has given her child (without legal sanction) to be raised by an aunt. While the worker might interpret the mother's act and the emotions accompanying it as a kind of sociopathic neglect, it may rather be operation of the institution, common in many black communities of fosterage.[19] The intrapsychic model of counseling leads one to peer into the murk of the psyche for the answer when one should be looking in the light provided by the culture.

The professional model and ideology of service coincides with organizational assumptions at many junctures. The maintenance of role distance between client and worker, the supposed cultural neutrality of technologies of help (behavior modification, the studied and "benign" inequality between worker and client in terms of self-disclosure, behavioral options, and power), and the monocultural/ linguist based of professional intervention all may work to produce tension and discomfort in some client/worker crosscultural transactions.[20]

The effect of these and other factors is to undermine the basic and important service these agencies can provide. Families under stress, ridden with conflict, making abortive attempts to resurrect themselves, can be restored to functional stability and vitality with help. However, if the agency and its services are uninformed about the political factors that oppress these families, the cultural expression of family structure and process, the social and cultural resources available to the family, and the cultural meaning of the problem and of help, then the agencies' efforts to intervene, however well-intentioned, may falter and sputter.

Child Welfare Services

One could reasonably argue that all services aimed at preserving, restoring, or creating family stability and integrity are child welfare services. However, we intend these services to include foster care, adoption, institutional and group care, child advocacy, child care services, juvenile justice services, and child protective service. We cannot discuss or review all these here, but the observations we make about some apply to others to one extent or another.

Child welfare services are both public and private (sometimes a mixture of both) and involve all the purposes Kadushin has outlined: support, supplement, and substitution. The federal government provides the organizational umbrella for many of these services. Most of the services are articulated through two offices: the Office of Human Development Services and the Social Security Administration. These two fall under the administration of the Department of Health and Human Services (formerly the Department of Health, Education, and Welfare).[21]

The principle program unit within the Office of Human Development Services is the Administration for Children, Youth, and Families. The Administration provides a range of services through its various components, including support of adequate developmental services for young children receiving out-of-home care during the day, advocacy for the needs of children, special adoption programs designed to facilitate the adoption of hard-to-place and special children, the development of model legislation for states in these areas, and the planning and coordination of, and provision of information for, programs related to the prevention and treatment of domestic violence.[22]

The Social Security Administration is responsible for the administration of the financial portion of AFDC, and through Title XX of the Act a variety of social services are provided to low-income families through a combination of state and federal monies, administered by the states and provided for by the Social Security Amendments of 1974.[23] (From fiscal year 1982-1983 the federal portion of the money will be provided to the states through block grants).

Of course, many children live in families who receive Old Age Survivors and Disability Insurance and, thus, Social Security provides supplementary services beyond AFDC and Title XX. The fact that the great bulk of child welfare services exist under governmental auspices means that many of the families of concern in this book are the responsibility of state public welfare/child welfare agencies.

Besides the social services arrayed under Title XX and the financial ministrations of AFDC, the three largest service areas are foster care, adoption services, and protective services. Under oppressive social conditions, the tissue that holds families together can become brittle, in spite of the best efforts to repair it. Eventually, it may tear. Then substitutive services, like foster care and adoption, intended to provide in extreme conditions, which provoke a temporary or permanent dissolution of the family, a substitute parent/child role system, become extremely important for the socialization and development of children. Yet, as Billingsley and Giovannoni point out black children (and their point applies to other minority children) are seriously underrepresented in the most desirable, developmentally appropriate substitutive services, namely, foster home placement and adoption. Unfortunately, they are overrepresented in the least desirable: institutional settings.[24] The situation has not changed substantially since the authors wrote in the mid-1970s. Two trends, one mired in controversy, may, however, help in reversing this trend: transracial adoption and permanency planning.

Transracial adoption arouses conflicting and competing emotions, but given the inability of adoption agencies to reach into minority communities with any consistent effectiveness and the disproportionate numbers of minority children dependent on services outside the family, transracial adoption is seen by some, at the least, as a temporary measure. Others judge it to be a legitimate though difficult choice to be made regarding the ultimate future of minority kids.[25] At the heart of the controversy is a version of the issue at the center of this book: Can effective socialization of minority children occur within the dominant cultural environment? Will transracial adoption produce minority children who are truly marginal people with no deep cultural roots and with a thorough rift in their personal identity? We can only agree that the relationship between identity and culture is fateful, but given insufficient numbers of minority adoptive families (which is more apparent than real), one cannot be too sanguine about the viability of, say, a residential institution as a fertile field for breeding identities suffused with ethnic pride. There are agencies, too few, specializing, for example, in the placement of black children with black families and providing a range of services for black families and children. They may never be sufficient in number until there are supporting social policies seriously addressing the problems of deprivation and discrimination as they affect family life and until there are policies that recognize that the world of black, brown, red, and yellow children is as real as that of white kids.

The point of permanency planning is to periodically review, via a panel of professionals, workers, and citizens, the progress and status of all children receiving foster care services from the State.[26] That these children have quality of care, continuity of care, and as permanent an environment of socialization (including returning to the biological family) as possible is the ultimate goal of the planning team. The spur to such planning is the knowledge that far too many children within the child welfare system (again, minority children suffer more than their share in this regard) have become nomads, moving silently from placement to placement, never finding the stability so essential to salubrious development. This nomadism is especially true of children six years and older.[27]

But in spite of these developments substitutive services such as these embody typical and distressing defects: repudiation of the value of minority families and communities, for example the failure to involve minorities in development and maintenance of programs and policies that directly affect them and the assumption of pathology in the family system as a whole; inability to incorporate the knowledge of the damage that racism and poverty do to families in the delivery of services; ignorance of minority culture, for example the failure to employ the extended family as a kind of substitutive service; the organizational distance (geographical and philosophical) between the agency and the community; and the perception of deviant behavior as causal rather than social, economic, or political oppression.[28]

Children who are abused and neglected constitute, tragically, a rapidly increasing subpopulation of all children.[29] And, once again, low-income and minority children are overrepresented in this unfortunate sample. As a nation we have become aroused and aware of this problem over the last ten years. Techniques for assessing and intervening into family abuse and neglect have become more sophisticated and our knowledge of the factors involved in the perpetration of abuse and neglect more sensitive and complex. However, for culturally different children two beliefs continue to affect their fates and the fates of their families.

First, the abuse and neglect of children by parents suggests the inadequacy and emotional disturbance of parents. For low-income minority parents such a suggestion may be a foregone conclusion. Removal of the children from the home, given this kind of assessment, becomes a preferred strategy (although this predilection has been under some attack recently).[30] Secondly, many cases of abuse and neglect are difficult to define. When the agency suspects pathology and maltreatment, it may ignore the possibility that it is witness to culturally different standards of child-rearing.

This is not to imply that any culture encourages cruelty to children but to point out that not all cases are clear-cut and that the data that informs the assessment in these cases may be deficient and distorted where it lacks cultural awareness. In addition, the decision to remove a child from the home does not simply turn on the evaluation of destructive or insensitive behavior of the parents. The social context of that behavior is critical to the evaluation. If the evaluation is bereft of cultural knowledge it is skewed and incomplete. Finally, there is generally thought to be a relationship between the degree of social and economic stress applied to a family and the likelihood of abusive behavior. Low-income minority families face more than their share of oppressive environmental conditions, and this must be acknowledged, as well as the families' attempts to cope, as part of any complete assessment.[31]

In summary, the complex and sometimes confused network of family and child services is important to minority children. Their over-representation in low-income and poverty populations means that they, as a group, will face extraordinary risks in development and maturation. The agencies that attempt to serve them sometimes ignore the character of these risks in their philosophies and methods of service and sadly do not reach or provide the quality of care needed by these risk-prone children and families. A significant element in the failure of these agencies is the lack of social support and encouragement to do what may need to be done to provide adequate service. Also, the failure may lie with the assumptions that fund service delivery, namely the bureaucratic and professional ideologies. However, the most poignant reason for whatever failures there are may be the deficiency in acknowledging the cultural environs in which these children and families live.

To discover culture is not to discover panaceas. The problems are there; they are complex, and many are unregenerate. However, if they are to yield to our ministrations and policies, our efforts must not only be emboldened by ethical commitment but by genuine understanding and not just the artful but often inaccurate assumptions of pathology.

A SAMPLER OF MYTHS ABOUT MINORITY CULTURES: CHILD-REARING AND FAMILY LIFE

As we have insisted at several points in this book, we cannot dismiss the destruction that racism and discrimination wreak. Concerning cultural matters, one of the most corrupt acts of racism is to create an artifice of belief about minority cultures to justify and rationalize shabby, disreputable treatment. Such myths here and there may be laced with reality, but more generally, these myths are a congeries of belief, inference, and judgment serving two basic purposes. Obviously, they shore up and encapsulate the sanctity of dominant culture and social structure (as much as the myths about the atavistic qualities of slaves supported the lucrative economy and rickety ethics of plantation society). Thus, normative standards are stabilized by pointing the finger at deviations from them.[32] Furthermore, these myths allow a continuing condemnation and commination of minority cultures disguised by polite and scientifically neutral jargon, for example the culture of poverty. Such myths abet injustice and maltreatment where the frank confrontation of them would be a source of embarrassment and a breeding ground for dialectical and political tension, leading perhaps to some resolution (de Tocqueville and Myrdal, both insightful outsiders, made such an observation).[33] On the other hand, we must be cautious here. In the attempt to correct pernicious mythology and hoping to set the record somewhat straight we may inadvertently be a party to the imaginative creation of other myths. We hope not.

The Tangle of Pathology

A beguiling phrase (and epithet), *the tangle of pathology*, comes from the U.S. Department of Labor report on the black family in 1965 (the *Moynihan Report*), and it continues to haunt our thinking about poor black families. While it may evoke vivid imagery, it is a perturbation of facts and supports the notion that somehow (The history of slavery? The tribal African past?) black culture and society are flawed.*

In this view, family and personal disorganization among lower-income blacks — educational failures, low occupational achievement, the high incidence of crimes against persons and property, divorce, and illegitimacy — are all in some way the creation of a lifestyle that lacks sufficient motivating imagery and normative principle to ensure stability, achievement, conformity, and integration with the larger culture. The source of this cultural inadequacy is the family, and the victim of it is the black male and his role as breadwinner and provider. Made inert by a lack of motivation and skill and overwhelmed by the matriarchal emasculation of his identity as a male, the low-income black male can only flounder in the stiff competition of the job market. Failures there only compound a life of personal disorganization further tearing at the fabric of family life and further ensuring the supremacy of the female, thus inviting more destruction of male competence, and so it goes.[34]

For Hispanic families a similar myth prevails. Its essence is that the traditional Hispanic family (primarily Mexican-American in this case) houses values and practices anathema to achievement and accomplishment and the eventual frustrations there lead to personal and social disorganization. Examples of these subversive (to economic advancement and status acquisition) values are emphasis on the present, conformity to family norms rather than the norm of achievement, and distrust of nonfamilial relationships.[35]

The idea of the web of pathology ensnaring these families is another version of the idea of the *culture of poverty* (although, implicitly, these criticisms suggest the *poverty of minority culture*). Such a notion recognizes the hardships that poverty brings, but it also suggests that the grinding conditions of poverty over generations produce a culture common to all who are poor that works to prevent all but the most clever members of that culture from escaping their condition.[36] This conceptual scheme gained such currency in the 1960s that it was widely thought, though the practice was obscure, that the only reasonable tack to take in fighting poverty was to fight the culture that poverty wrought and that proved to be such a drag on achievement and upward mobility. (The Head Start program, for all its

---

*Our thinking about middle-class blacks may be tempered by our assumptions that they have become more "respectable" (more like us in their approval of middle-class values and lifestyles).

good, was predicated on such a notion.)

In recent years, there has been a reaction to this belief, at least in the academic world and among minority authors,[37] but the operating assumptions of the idea continue to fuel our efforts to understand and provide service to families and children of these cultures. And the truth *is* hard to pull clear from the statistics that appear to support the tangle-of-pathology hypothesis. Minorities *do* suffer higher recorded rates of illegitimacy, broken families, low educational, and occupational achievement (and the rest of the litany of social ills). However, it is exceedingly difficult to determine the extent to which these phenomena issue from the personal and familial burden of living on the margin economically and socially. It is our view that the widely advertised (and they are seen and recorded through white eyes) multiple pathologies occur *in spite of* minority culture and *not because of it.* For many members of minority culture the streets are mean and the money is lean. Given that, minorities must develop patterns of response and adaptation that allow them to cope with and detoxify the poisonous effects of social injustice, institutional and individual racism, and attacks on self-esteem.[38] That these invidious social forces do not cause more damage than they do is a tribute to the resilience and resonance of minority cultures.

Hyman Rodman once posed an interesting and plausible hypothesis designed to synthesize the theory of the culture and poverty and the realities of racism and deprivation. He speculated that the destruction of the breadwinner role (through economic conditions and errant social policies) in the ghetto and barrio stimulated the development of adaptive strategies meant to sustain family life and continuity. While a variety of moral agents and observers — social workers, teachers, police, academicians, etc. — might regard these strategies as expressions of a deviant culture, Rodman thought that, given the existing conditions, they were eminently suitable for coping. These adaptive efforts were not cultural per se but instead resulted from the stretching of preferred values in the service of stability and getting on.[39]

To regard low-income minority families and individuals as creating some misshapen and gross cultural environment of pathology is to ignore, at least, two important facts: most families in ghettos and barrios and rural pockets of poverty are intact (in 1974, around 65 percent of all black families in poverty were intact; the percentage was higher for Hispanics) with one or both parents working and the children attending school[40]; and one-parent families (solo mother) are not necessarily unhealthy (about 35 percent of all black families in poverty are female headed and they comprise slightly over one-half of all black families in poverty; for Hispanics, in 1974, the percentage of female-headed households was 17 percent),[41] most are not on welfare (2/3), and beyond the statistic of illegitimacy (which places them in the unstable category) they seem to be functioning as well as can be expected, considering the vagaries of the job market for females. In other words, these families, *in terms of the provision of continuity and stability,* are much more often like us than different from (and deviant compared to) the rest of us. This is not to gloss over the daily struggles they face but to affirm that families in poverty manage to stay together in some form and raise children with some dignity and aplomb.

Cultural Deprivation

We have already alluded to this myth. As indicated in the opening chapter, to suggest that one culture is valid and rich and another is invalid and barren can only be done in ignorance of the meaning of culture. To repeat briefly, culture is a fiction (*fictio,* in the classical sense, meaning something made), fashioned over time, providing its members with structures of meaning and coherence for all human activity, from the smallest personal gesture (a wink, say) to the grandest national gesture ("saving face," perhaps). Culture runs deep in the stream of our consciousness.[42] To suppose that a culture is deprived is to confuse culture with the social tools and resources required for competent societal membership. (William Ryan once suggested that instead of regarding the children of the barrio and ghettos as culturally deprived when they enter the public school system we ought to judge the school, an essential social resource, as deprived because it steadfastly refuses to recognize the reality and truth of the cultures of these children.[43]) The supposition of deprivation can only be spoken, too, from an ethnocentric platform; how else could we label a culture as lacking if it were not from the smug vantage point of superiority? Countless tales, some apocryphal, some not, spice anthropologists' accounts of their own and others' ethnocentric blinders, the blinders that allow us to teeter on the brink of regurgitation while watching a "primitive" devour dog meat while our own chops might drool over the prospect of snacking on the underside of that dirty, dumb bird, the turkey.

To capture the essence of these mistaken views of the relative superiority of cultures, reverse the situation for a moment. One could, with some justification (as James Meyer[44] once did) regard suburban middle-class culture as deprived, an environment in which there is a paucity of lingual or cultural variety, no sense of neighborhood or community, and where the nuclear family is adrift on its own. In Meyer's words, "Suburbia's children are living and learning in a land of distorted values and faulty perceptions. They have only the slightest notion of others; they judge them on the basis of suburban standards (such as 'cleanliness' or 'niceness'), generalize about groups on the basis of the few they might have known, and think in stereotypes."[45] This is perhaps true; however, is culture at fault or is it a problem of realizing a more effulgent cultural expression in an environment dunned by mobility, competition, achievement, and social distance? The point is we must be careful in our thinking about the relationship of social resources to cultural patterns of behavior and belief.

Let us not fool ourselves about cultural deprivation. More than any statistic that is able, the revelations of sensitive observers (like Robert Coles) capture the richness and complexity of other cultures, even those beseiged by economic and social oppression. Thomas Cottle, a white, Harvard-educated psychiatrist spent two years visiting with two children in Roxbury, a largely black, low-income community in the Boston area. Cottle's relationship with these two children was touchy at times but productive, thanks to his gentleness and fairness, and the childrens' basic honesty gave insights sufficient to underscore the point about the vitality of cultures as opposed to the poverty of social conditions, again and again. An example: "Yet again, the issue of poverty affects this development of the will. For children like Adrien and William D., who have received great quantities of love, have known nothing that resembles the idyllic setting where free play is possible day in and day out. And while their own style of play and work has developed in them wills of firmness as well as resiliency, they will be hard-pressed, as the years go on, to combat the feelings of self-doubt which almost every social institution will instill in them."[46] And, later, on the conflict of cultures, "Adrien and

William D. hold back anger from me partly because for them I am, along with others, a symbol of the culture that constrains. . . . More than just what they say or what I say, it is the encounter, the two cultures coming together to yield words, ideas, and passions that predominate."[47]

If it were only so, that the meeting of cultures would be grounded in hard-won but genuine respect and trust in the relationship between the institutions meant to support and repair family life and these children. Unfortunately, the attitude of these institutions is often of such a character that it separates and rends, and in such cases one can only be glad that their culture provides these children with a cushion, a respite. "Children of poverty, like children of any group destined to be kept from the center of society and hence from its protective rights and shelters, learn the language and value systems of two cultures, their own and the culture that withholds from them. These children in our country — economically deprived as they are, but who speak two languages, Spanish *and* English, Portugese *and* English, Italian *and* English, Yiddish *and* English, or one of the numerous Native American languages *and* English — represent the complex and rich inheritance which is theirs."[48] Cultural deprivation? No. Cultural difference? Yes.

Machismo and Matriarchy

Probably no ethnocentric epithet has had as much impact or fostered more misunderstanding than the idea of machismo. The dominant culture's conception of macho (as well as its commercial distortion) and its place in Hispanic cultures is probably as germane to those cultures as the ways in which Texans concoct chili is to its Mexican forebears.

Social scientists, journalists, and more casual observers frequently lay the sins of social disorganization among Hispanics at the feet of the Hispanic male and his presumed obsession with machismo and the behavior and attitudes it inspires. The usual view of machismo has several aspects:

1. While the imagery and symbolism of machismo has been around for generations (and, generally, has referred to the rights and obligations of the male head of the family, a conception quite sober in its implications), its current usage suggests

that the Hispanic male's frequently inferior social status generates in him a sometimes perverse, occasionally brutalizing strengthening of his authoritarian status within the family circle.[49]

2. The establishment and maintenance of the Hispanic male's authority in the family gives rise to such cultural esoterica as wife beating, child abuse, heavy drinking, philandering, the obsession with conception (as a sign of virility), and incessant boasting and preening.[50]

3. These male behaviors destroy the warp of family integrity, undermining the adequate socialization of children and their health as well, keep women psychologically, if not physically, incapable of caring for themselves and their children and lead, in the end, to the breakup of many family units.[51]

4. Devotion to machismo perpetuates the cycle of poverty. Male children are psychologically crippled because of inappropriate male models who encourage a compensatory need — in male children — to assume a compulsively masculine role. This role is so distorted and based on such a sense of inferiority that as adults, males cannot compete in the world of the marketplace and work.[52]

5. Machismo is a deeply embedded and normative part of most Hispanic cultures and, thus, at the core of the Hispanic male psyche.

This interpretation of machismo seems to lead us to the belief that because of the distortions of the gender roles in the Hispanic family, that family cannot but be a small ecology of pathology.

For black Americans an equally dangerous myth lurks about: the illusion of black matriarchy. According to his piece of ethnocentric fiction, the gender roles of adults in the family, like the Hispanic, are perverted.

The higher percentage of female-headed households in the black community (lower income especially) leads observers to suspect that more is operating here than just the collective misfortunes of divorce, desertion, premature death, and illegitimacy and that black culture has inherent within it a tendency toward family matriarchy (governance and rule of the family organization by the female) inviting oppression of the black male (though the rapidly increasing numbers of female-headed households in the white community does not seem to inspire the same trepidations about matriarchy).[53]

The maternal hegemony in black families effectively serves to psychically emasculate black males adding psychological insult to economic injury and leaving black males less capable than their nonblack peers of competing for job market dollars and opportunities.

The matriarchal structure of the family creates a pattern of socialization for males that seriously impedes the formation of solid male identifications and, therefore, male identity. The upshot is, of course, bizarre and pathological expressions of compensatory maleness.[54]

The black woman, especially the lower-income black woman, has become, in our thought, a Herculean figure possessing inordinate wisdom, Olympian power, and satanic cunning (the underside of this romanticism is that the black woman is immoral, castrating, and far from the pretty (and petty?) ideal of American femininity.[55]

So the cultural urge toward matriarchy (from distant African past, it is sometimes supposed) has driven the black family of the lower class and created generations of black males incapable of sustaining familial fidelity and occupational stability. An imposing piece of human statuary, the black matriarch has been hoist with her own petard, doomed to spare survival because of the subversion of her male's strength.

Are these myths really harmful and don't they contain a grain of truth? Yes is the answer to both questions. In terms of the damage they do, at the very least, these myths paint a false picture of minority family life and child-rearing practices, a picture that makes anything but the most dramatic measures seem inadequate to the task of helping these families. Those who deliver services and who provide supportive and supplemental care may be hesitant to take on the minority family precisely because of the enormity of the difficulties that may seem a matter of cultural pathogenesis — difficulties hardly to be eased by the unguents of family therapy, child advocacy, or home-care services. The culture of minorities becomes, then, something scary — to be avoided if possible — or, if need be, to be tamed only by the broadcast policy strokes (crackdowns on crime and errant welfare fathers, cutting back benefits, or removing children from their homes). At the extreme, these myths encourage social policies that directly affect these families by denying them the social resources they need to redress and compensate for the inequities they face daily. Once again, the *Moynihan Report* illuminates this often insidious process. It cited "numerous figures on illegitimate Negro children, broken homes, lack of education, crime, narcotic addiction, and so on. It charts Negro unemployment, but not once does it suggest national action to crack down on discrimination by labor unions. Instead, it insists that massive federal action must be initiated to correct the matriarchal structure of the Negro family."[56] Social policies possessing such a mythical base spew forth programs fateful for minorities and are the stuff of which "the folklore of white supremacy"[57] is made. They continue, and they justify ethnocentrism and discrimination and result in a poverty of ideas and action that might substantially defuse the interethnic and cultural tensions underlying socioeconomic disparities.

THE REALITY

Is there a basis in truth? Certainly. All myths and all stereotypes are caricatures of a truth, a limited truth that they artfully extend and embellish. The destructiveness lies in the degree of distortion, the misinterpretation of a social, economic, or political fact as a cultural one (assuming that machismo, for example, rather than job discrimination destroys the breadwinner role), and the assumption, deeply embedded in the core of these myths, that a cultural system would produce generations of maladaption and disorganization is an insult.

There is, of course, legitimate disagreement among authors and observers about the shape and extensiveness of particular cultures. There is even disagreement about whether black Americans and Hispanic Americans have a distinct culture at all. We believe that minority culture, though suffused with the pigment of the dominant culture, is real. Failure to recognize this will continue to hamper, even in the best of times, efforts to provide adequate service and resources to these groups. Objections to the belief that minorities of color possess a culture are important and should be addressed.

These objections can be broken into four basic arguments:

1. Highlighting cultural differences as implicated in the problems minority groups contend with tends to distract attention from the social forces undermining the life chances of these groups, and thus acts as an excuse for inaction in the area of compensatory justice or the provision of social resources. In fact, emphasis on the debilitating aspects of culture has been one of the traditional means of blaming the victim.

2. Culture is too often erroneously implicated in the interpretation of the demographic ills besetting minority populations (crime rates, poor population health, etc.).

3. Supports of the idea of cultural differences and the centrality of cultural conflict, it is argued, mistakenly assume for each group a single cultural canopy under which each group member stands. Thus, they ignore the richness and diversity within cultures and the cultural differences within similar ethnic groups, Hispanics, for example.

4. Assuming culture as the centerpiece of understanding and helping minorities in need obscures the importance of class. Many patterns of living and enduring complexes of behavior may bear more relationship to class than culture or, to put it slightly differently, it may be that class has produced a more distinctive culture than ethnicity (to wit: white and black middle class supposedly share a more common life-style than black middle-class and black lower-class individuals).

These arguments must be taken seriously. Considering children and families, we would respond to them summarily in this way: Knowing a group is culturally different does *not* explain high rates, say, of family disorganization. If anything, it helps explain *how* many families maintain considerable integrity in the face of social and economic oppression. While there may be noticeable differences across class lines in child-rearing practices, when blacks or Hispanics cross those lines, moving upward, they do not automatically surrender those styles of being a family and raising children. Rather, what they face is considerably more pressure from the outside toward the infusion of the dominant culture. Still, in a given Hispanic family, the demarcation of gender roles might remain even though they were ascending the class ladder. What this family would face is a dialectical tension between what has been practiced and prized and, now, what seems to be expected. Over generations such a tension would yield a normative drift (to the dominant practices), but the distinctive Hispanic flavor of life would be evident.[58]

It is obvious, too, that no monolithic culture stands implacably as a foundation for each of the groups of our concern here. For Hispanics, though there are common threads throughout, sufficient differences exist between various groups to regard them as unique subcultures, maybe even separate ethnic groupings. Mexicans, Puerto Ricans, Cubans, and South Americans of various kinds are very different, yet the fiber of cultural similarity runs through them all: the importance of both supernatural and natural systems of defining illness and healing or the strong devotion to their language, all so similar etymologically and a meaty part of their orientation to the world.[59] The persistence of their native tongue, their past history of resilience in the face of conquering alien cultures confronts Hispanics (notably Mexican-Americans) with the continuing dilemma of biculturalism. *Mestizaje* (the result of the crossbreeding between the Indians — the race — and their Spanish conquerors) implies that Mexicans have a long tradition of synthesis and tension in this area.[60] Parenthetically, but importantly, it should be noted that biculturalism is not assimilation, nor is it quiet coexistence between one culture and another. Instead, ". . . it is an often tense, irresoluble, mental juggling of clashing elements of two cultures."[61] So we caution child welfare and family service agencies that working with a Cuban is not the same as working with a Mexican-American but suggest that there are enough common cultural elements that learning about one culture is learning something about the other. Though the days, hopefully, are gone when you can humiliate or beat the culture out of an "alien," we should be aware that the tension of biculturalism can be a significant impediment for Hispanic clients trying to live on the margin and keep family together.

For black Americans, questions about culture are different. Many who observe, write about, or live as black citizens are unsure about the reality and palpability of black culture. From Frazier[62] on, many authors have been skeptical of the idea of African cultural roots and, because of that, are suspicious of the idea of a genuine black culture.[63] Others believe in black culture but only as an inchoate mass, a conglomerate of the dominant culture, regional and dialect differences, adaptive styles rooted in slavery and generations of discrimination, and "put-ons," but a culture without a solid core, linguistically or symbolically.[64]

Still others insist there is a core black culture that bears little resemblance to anything African, past or present. Gwaltney suggests, "Core black culture is more than ad hoc synchronic adaptive survival. Its values, systems of logic and world view are rooted in a lengthy peasant tradition and clandestine theology. It is the notion of sacrifice for kin, the belief in the natural sequence of cause and effect — 'Don't nothin'' go over the devil's back but don't bind him under the belly' — It is a classical restricted notion of the possible. It esteems the deed more than the wish, venerates the 'natural man' over the sounding brass of technology and the wit to know that 'Everybody talking 'bout Heaven ain't goin' there.' "[65]

It is our view then that while there are critical differences between Hispanic groups, there is a ligature of commonality, and there is something like a core black culture; it may not have quite the internal force of Hispanic cultures, but parts of it are as recognizable to the denizens of Watts as to those of Monroe County. It is true that not all (or even most) efforts to cope with racism or discrimination or poverty end up as elements of culture. They are, instead, what they seem, attempts to survive in an insensitive world, and each of these cultural expressions is, in some way, an amalgam of some aspects of the dominant culture.

So culture is real, as are cultural differences. Where there are differences, there is ample opportunity for misunderstanding, conflict, and destructiveness. Cultures are articulated through communication, they meet through communication, and the conflict that may erupt when they meet can be resolved through communication. And the lingua franca of any cross-cultural meeting is understanding.

FAMILIES AND CHILDREN

Culture and ethnicity so shape the lives of parents, children, and professionals that the two become a dimension of learning and development. To better understand the child and the family, we need to understand the cultural baggage that the child brings to the school, the preschool, or agency setting. Without understanding the culture of the child and family, and how it diverges from values and culture of public institutions, it will be difficult for professionals of the institutions to meet the child's needs. Inability to understand children of varying cultures will make it difficult for professionals to understand either the child's learning or growth, or his family's ability or inability to cope.[66]

In the spirit of Seelig's words we would like to explore some truths about black and Hispanic families and children — truths to combat the widespread egregious errors of the myths we explored earlier.

The Extended Family

Increasing urbanization, the influence of pop culture, social mobility, and increasing and persistent economic pressures have placed the extended family in jeopardy. Today, the nuclear family, in its various forms, would seem to be both the statistical and cultural norm. But for many blacks and Hispanics the extended family is not only a real and vibrant cultural expression but an important adaptive and life-preserving institution.

THE BLACK EXTENDED FAMILY. The extended family is a genealogical reality based on bilateral descent primarily and marriage and fosterage secondarily. This kin network provides material and symbolic resources, entails clear obligations, and enhances chances for biological survival.[67] In addition, in the rural South, the extended family offers an important support and mechanism for migration to the urban North and West. Extended family relations may continue, in one form or another, long after the migration.

Besides as a statement of continuity in the midst of social change, and the fertilization of generational roots, the extended family is frequently essential as a socioeconomic unit in an environment of deprivation and uncertainty. Cooperation, sharing of resources and responsibilities, resource development, crisis management, and socialization (social control, too) are accomplished within the extended kin network. Perhaps the most important function of the extended family, however, is the responsibility for children, providing for their material as well as spiritual needs. And when, for whatever reason (though it is frequently medical or economic), a parent can no longer adequately care for a child, the extended family may function structurally as a parental surrogate.[68] Thus appears one of the most observed and often misunderstood practices of the kin network: *fosterage.* Failure of the natural parents to perform their roles may lead them to give the child to another adult(s), usually a relative or sometimes a friend, with the expectation that the surrogates will assume full and competent socialization of the child. Fosterage most often takes place within the web of the extended family, among its members, that is. In the event of fosterage, the natural rights of the parent will not be denied.[69] In some cases, particularly urban areas, the child may actually be in the same dwelling as the natural parent.[70]

Fosterage is based on the prevalent belief that the raising of children is an obligation of kinship and where child-keeping occurs it is a highly cherished right.[71] The practice of fosterage conflicts with legal definitions of parental rights and responsibilities, but the importance of the extended family exerts pressure for the nonjural definition.[72] Whatever else its origin and rationale, fosterage assures that in times of socioeconomic stress, children will be nurtured within a familiar context.

The origins of the extended family in the black community are unclear, but its place in the pastiche of culture is unmistakable. Even when nuclear families have achieved financial independence there is great pressure to remain, at least symbolically, within the fold of the extended kinship grouping.[73]

Some of the structural aspects (not thoroughly agreed upon) of the extended family include the following:

1. a core group of adults, often four generations and frequently including the "founders" of the family
2. a generational structure of elderly persons (the founders), middle-aged siblings (and sometimes cousins) and their spouses (the nucleus families), the married children and grandchildren of these families (who may form independent households, subextended families, but who are felt to be part of the core family), and various mobile individuals (children, adolescents, and adults who may traverse between households in response to a variety of needs and pressures)[74]
3. economic, social, and emotional interdependency — relatives relying upon one another for an array of supports
4. a common geographic base (and usually a high degree or propinquity) so that even when members move away their hearts often remain firmly grounded in the core region
5. frequent visiting and interaction between members
6. usually a dominant figure (ordinarily one of the founders)

whose home is regarded as a base for family operations[75]

As we indicated earlier, a primary function of the extended kin group is the care and feeding of its children. The value of motherhood and children cannot be overestimated, and the extended family takes pride in the fact that "we take care of our own." Underlying this is the singular importance of consanguinity as compared to conjugal ties. Aschenbrenner offers that this may be in part because conjugal relationships are much more sensitive, therefore susceptible, to economic pressures, pressures that can be more readily absorbed within the consanguine network.[76]

While there is debate about the degree to which the extended family exists beyond the rural South, there is enough evidence to consider it as an important social institution, though, perhaps, transformed in critical ways, in the urban North and West.[77] In any event, we ". . . must, therefore, be careful not to minimize the importance of kinship among clients. Caseworkers have been prone to deal with individuals, and more recently with people-in-families, but what Leichter and Mitchell's (1967) findings suggest is that among those Jewish clients — and perhaps among other social groups — the approach should be to try to work with them as people-in-kin-groups."[78]

THE HISPANIC EXTENDED FAMILY. Though there is disagreement about the importance or pervasiveness of the extended family among Hispanics ("No convincing evidence has been found to support the notion that the Spanish-speaking/surnamed family is extraordinarily familistic, extended, and patriarchal."[79]), there is evidence that the extended family remains at least conceptually an important structural element in Hispanic cultures.[80] Such a conglomerate of kin seems to be essential in the lives of rural Hispanics; those living in cities find it more difficult to maintain the tradition in the face of a more complex, rapid pace of life.[81]

The core of the extended family for some Hispanic groups is the *compadrazgo* (co-parent) relationship. Traditionally of a religious orientation compadrazgo refers to the relationship formed when friends of the family become godparents (*padrino/madrina*) and sponsors of the child at baptism. The person then becomes a *comadre* or *copadre* (co-mother or co-father) with the parents of the child and not only assumes a range of defined responsibilities but maintains a regular relationship with the child's family. Among urban and socially mobile Hispanics the compadrazgo relationship may be diluted, the godparent may not have formally defined and structurally provided responsibilities for example, but the spirit and symbolism of it remains.[82] The relationships that evolve from the compadrazgo system can become enormously complicated but form the superstructure of the extended family.

As is the case with the extended kin system in the black American world, the system among Hispanics involves shared responsibilities, mutual support, a kind of symbolic adhesive keeping together a large number of individuals in a coherent framework of meaning, maintenance, and stability. For Hispanics, the extended family structure may not have the clear relationship to economic survival that it does in black communities but it probably has a more institutionalized and specific religious definition and sanction.

Some of the central aspects of the Hispanic versions of the extended family may include the following:

1. an enduring respect for the authority of the father who reigns supreme over the household (and in more traditional families has somewhat more freedom and responsibility than the mother; this may also be the basis of the genuine idea of machismo)
2. a sturdy and abiding love for the mother who clearly plays the major expressive, integrative role in the family
3. the formalized copadre/comadre relationship that reiterates and supports the parental role distinctions described above
4. deep loyalty to the family above and beyond other social institutions[83]

Some observers of Hispanic culture suggest that Hispanics, because of their strong commitment to language and cultural heritage, confront, especially in urban areas or among the new middle class, a daily battle between more traditional values and practices and the beliefs and behavior patterns of the dominant culture. On the traditional side, we might expect to find a strong commitment to familism, the extended family structure, a relaxed patriarchy, a restrained attitude toward the stresses and crises of daily life, a stronger belief in folk medicine and healing (*curanderismo*), and firmly defined, discrete gender roles.[84] The dialectic is joined by the incursion of contemporary middle-class values into traditional territory (for instance a more egalitarian gender division of labor, more reliance on impersonal and bureaucratic social institutions, and the ascent of the nuclear family).[85] The conflict here is much like, in both character and seriousness, the distinction reported by Holtzman et al. in a study of anglo families in Texas and families in Mexico.[86] The inferences Holtzman draws about the differences between these two populations are instructive for understanding the dilemmas some Hispanics face when they migrate to the United States. "Mexico is poorer in physical resources; for that reason the Mexican believes that his determination and his efforts is [sic] not enough, that before and above man there are given conditions — providential he would call them — which are difficult or impossible to set aside. This makes him a skeptic, distrustful of action, a believer in forces superior to himself, more likely to cavil than act."[87] Ignoring the negative intonation given this observation and recognizing that Mexican-Americans who have been in the United States for some time do not necessarily reflect this orientation to the world outside themselves, we can, however, see the enormous cultural pressures on Mexican-Americans who are recent migrants to this society. The cultural belief systems stand starkly opposite.

Whatever we choose to highlight about Hispanic cultures, we cannot ignore the cultural importance of the language and the tenacity of the native tongue. If language is the major vehicle for transporting cultural baggage then we can understand why many Hispanics are determinedly, though tensely, bicultural. For a number of Hispanics, perhaps more so for the upwardly mobile, bilingualism is problematic, and the problem often shows itself in parents' decision whether to teach their children Spanish or not. Such conflicts and the inevitable confusions of biculturalism have produced many accomplished bilingualists as well as a number of hybridized language forms, *pochismo* and *Spanglish* for example.[88] For children in school evidence of bilingual capacity should be cause for celebration, especially considering that so many Anglo children are artlessly monolingual. Unfortunately, for too many administrators and teachers, bilingualism seems cause for alarm. For a child struggling to become bilingual the implicit criticism of and overt attacks on the language (and, therefore, culture) confound the endeavor to form a coherent and resilient identity and often places the child at odds with his or her culture. Besides ethnic pride the tenacity of the language is probably, too, a function of social oppression, racism, and segregation and provides balm and continuity against the railing of hostile external forces.

We do not intend to paint an idyllic and rapturous scene of the families and children of minorities. As with all of us, there are ruptures and strains in the family circle and in the culture itself. How many of these are the product of socioeconomic pressures and how many of cultural pressures is difficult to assess. When Boulette[89] lists the emotional hazards that Hispanic children encounter, she attributes them to poverty and minority status but some she recounts (like faulty child-rearing practices) can only have some cultural content. It is our judgment that under the wrenching conditions of poverty and discrimination, cultural practices that ordinarily may have survival value under the stresses of deprivation within an "alien" society may become distended and misshapen. If it is a part of Hispanic culture to encourage the authority of the father, when that father is exposed to continuing unemployment, say, on top of institutional and personal racism, the effort to maintain the dignity of filial authority may, on some occasions, devolve into twisted attempts to sustain his prerogatives and responsibilities. Nevertheless the great majority of families are able to hold a pattern of stability, developmental nurturance, and generational continuity in spite of socioeconomic stress.[90] If anything comes through with clarity, it is the implacable devotion to their children that typifies these ethnic minority cultures.

THE ORGANIZATIONAL CONTEXT: MEDIUM FOR CULTURAL CONFLICT

In each of the chapters of this book, we have asserted that the organizational structure of program and service is no mere technological artifact or theoretical construct but a cultural invention as well. Organizations and the patterned activity they embody are imbued with values, symbols, structures of meaning, and normative patterns of activity.[91] To some degree, roughly speaking, the bureaucratic, professional culture shares the same heritage as elements of the dominant culture itself. Consequently, when a minority client enters the bureaucratic world of service he or she is confronting an environment rife with possibilities for conflict, misunderstanding, and tension.

Earlier in this chapter we identified some aspects of bureaucracy and the professional world as important constraints on the delivery of service. There is little or no possibility that these will disappear, in spite of continuing developments in organizational theory, but we must think clearly about their impact and the possibility of reshaping them to more adequately fit the circumstances that minority clients bring to the helping agency.[92]

As conceptions, bureaucracy and the ideology of profession share many attributes. Both assume the superiority of specialized knowledge and expertise (as opposed to common sense or folk wisdom), well-defined role distance between practitioner (or functionary) and consumer (or client), the importance of durable, clearly articulated rules, regulations, and roles (normative standards of performance and ethics versus situational flexibility and tolerance for uncertainty) to guide intervention and organizational activity, and the importance of controlling or ignoring the perimeters of uncertainty. As critical as these may be functionally, they can and do produce a number of "pathologies." The role distance and affective neutrality required of the bureaucrat can dissolve into dehumanization and insensitivity. The thick underbrush of rules and norms may lead to rigidity, a preference for order and normative propriety and so defeat the capacity to cope with puzzling and complex human problems. Rather than the idiosyncratic understanding of each individual instance, on occasion the need for preserving the autonomy of knowledge and the sanctity of the technical base of operations puts the burden of success on the responsiveness of the client rather than the pertinence of the knowledge.[93] Certainly knowledge and the technology it spawns must give the practitioner utility and confidence, but it must also provide a perspective that respects the nonrepeatable and unique dimensions of any situation.[94]

Although bureaucracies and professional norms have coincident assumptions, they also clash. The tension between the bureaucratic world and the professional role has been suspected for a long time. Conflicts between the hierarchy of authority and its demands and professional autonomy; the placing of organizational loyalty before client needs, the orientation to the goals of the organization rather than unblemished loyalty to the goals of service; the chasm between personal life and organization role; and the expectations among professionals that they must put the requirements of the professional ethic above personal need are some of the points of collision between the bureaucracy and the professions.[95]

The responsiveness of the professional helper to the ethnic minority client is sometimes confounded, then, by the assumptions of the bureaucratic model of service and the culture of the professional, as well as by the areas of tension between the two. The barriers to understanding are shored up by the obvious differences between the bureaucratic/professional ideologies, and those of other subcultures and cultures. To render the environment of service more hospitable to minority clients, at a minimum agencies must familiarize themselves with some cultural attributes standing in opposition to the professional/bureaucratic world.

Humanismo, Dignidad, and the Uniqueness of the Individual

The core black culture and Hispanic cultures all seem to place strong emphasis on the unique qualities of each individual — that particular alignment of traits and characteristics that makes him or her irreplaceable and an object of dignified treatment. The individual is presumed free to develop in his or her own way as long as that development does not encroach on another's freedom. The joy taken in children is in part the joy of watching a new and unique human being take a place in family and culture. Such respect for the individual does not conflict with but, rather, enhances the family communality we spoke of earlier; the family is the soil in which the individual blooms.[96] This regard for humanness (*humanismo*) may typically be thwarted by the pragmatic and impersonal character of the bureaucratic paradigm. Related to the value of the human being is the importance of maintaining and not assaulting the dignity of each person. One may argue with or oppose but under no circumstance should one subvert or torpedo the dignity of another. Losing face or implied anonymity in a public context is a devastating personal assault. Regrettably, many agency procedures and practices are implicitly built around the notion of case rather than person and the forced inanity of the designation.

Personalismo and Affective Existentialism

Hispanics prefer personal contact and individual attention in dealing with organizational structures. This is somewhat related to a preference for the affective side of interpersonal life and seems to have its counterpart in what Rose defines as the *affective existentalism* of the core black culture.[97] The intensity and persistence of the affective dimension of life may be related to the value of a shared history and common evolution as well as the effect of ethnic solidarity and pride. Dress, slang, the expressive ebullience of nicknames and names, humor, and touching and embracing (abrazos) all reflect the value placed upon the individual and solidify the expressive glue holding people together. To mispronounce, for example, a Puerto Rican's name is to commit a social offense and is an affront to the dignity of that individual.[98]

The Communal Basis of Life

"The Black culture stresses the uniqueness of the individual but at the same time must be concerned about the welfare and happiness of family and friends. Stress is placed on communal living and sharing. Although life is hard, one strives to balance the bitter and the sweet. Life cannot be taken too seriously because one may lose their [sic] purpose for existence in the first place."[99] In Hispanic cultures, *familismo,* the importance and centrality of family, seems an enduring part of culture. The obligations to and resources of the family are a proving ground for and provide nourishment of the self, especially during times of crisis.[100] Once again, many service agencies even though they may interview family members tend to take an individual adaptive approach to the resolution of problems, meaning that one individual is usually defined as the locus of problems or as bearing the brunt of family tensions and that the inherent resources of the family may be ignored. However, the virtual explosion of family therapies and theories in the last decade or so acts as a countervailing force to this tendency.

These are a few of the cultural values that may be foiled in bureaucratic client encounters. Where they are at serious odds with the professional bureaucratic culture, obstacles to the provision of service multiply.

CHANGING THE SERVICE ORGANIZATION:
THE PROVISION OF CULTURALLY RELEVANT HELP

Leininger observes that "In cultural contact situations, there is a tendency for the superior cultural group (by virtue of size, perceived status, and other factors) to impose its beliefs, practices, and values on a less dominant cultural group." This she calls *cultural imposition.*[101] In the health field, as an example, Leininger claims such an attitude leads to intense conflict in at least the following areas: the values surrounding health and health practices; the confrontation of technological neutrality with affective involvement; the clash of ethnocentric biases; and the views of health as they represent larger views of the universe (the critical cultural values).

The suggestions that follow are general in nature and are meant to recognize the diversity of family and child service agencies and to correct cultural imposition.

CHANGING PERSPECTIVES. Professions seem to prefer a kind of mechanistic, linear, sequential, causal thinking (the positivist paradigm). Not bad in itself, and certainly responsible for many improvements in helping technologies, this view of the world may at times be a hindrance to the provision of culturally relevant help. Such a model needs to be augmented with or replaced by an organic approach to understanding human problems, an approach presuming that human dilemmas and conflicts are ecological in nature, that is they involve the simultaneous interaction of culture, social institution, geography, family, mind, body, etc. We can, of course, never hope to really grasp the reticulate character of human acts and endeavors. However, we can appreciate, at the level of intuition at least, the web of circumstances enveloping us all. Organic thinking is holistic, intuitive, imagistic, empathic, spontaneous, and playful. It involves a kind of "combinatory play,"[103] the play of our senses over the convolutions and contours of a situation so that we may apprehend its complexity. This does not deny that there is a proper moment for analytic thinking. However, such a perspective is rarely taught to human service workers and administrators, and while the method of teaching it may be ambiguous, it seems essential for appreciating the resonant core of another culture.

CULTURAL LEARNING. To appreciate the topography of another culture we must feel it. Understanding a different culture is always difficult, and the learning that takes place is often no more than the affirmation of clumsy stereotypes. Frequently the learning provided is superficial (a four-hour workshop on Mexican-American culture is something to be sure, but it is not enough). Whatever learning we undergo must not just be didactic (the telling and recounting of various elements of another culture); it must as well be experiential and involve real encounters with culture — experiencing its smells, its sounds, its texture, its people, its humor, and the like. The human service worker must have the opportunity to be transported to that other culture, not only for the intellectual comprehension of it but for the human sense of it. We must speak the language of the culture. Hall and Whyte suggest the following about the executive in another culture: "Whatever background information he has, he needs to interpret to himself how people act *in relation to himself.* He is dealing with a cross-cultural situation. The link between two cultures is provided by acts of communication between the administrator, representing one culture, and people representing another."[104] Communication does not refer simply to language but also to the intricate expressions and affirmations of meaning that give a culture its vitality and atmosphere. There are now available models of cultural learning intent on just that sort of appreciation (the University of Hawaii, ensconced in a multicultural environment, has produced a series of monographs, videotapes, manuals, etc., aimed at promoting intercultural learning, and these are employable in a variety of contexts).[105]

ORGANIZATIONAL DIVERSITY. Organizations committed to hiring minority personnel can expect, in some instances, that those individuals will not be only workers and administrators but teachers as well. That is to say both ascribed (minority status) and achieved (administrative role) status can define the minority member's role in the organization. However, it is not to say that blacks, for example, must always define themselves in terms of their blackness or that it is incumbent on them to teach the majority. However, minorities within an organization can, with dignity, be assigned to promote cultural learning and respect, if they so choose. Learning, in these cases, will also occur through both the formal and informal contacts of organizational members who come from diverse cultural backgrounds. An organization with a heterogeneous, variegated population stands a better chance of attaining a level of cultural awareness than an organization stifled by homogeneity. While significant learning can be happenstance, a product of unplanned encounters, it is our view that the most effective way to promote intercultural sensitivity is through formalized, required cultural learning.

Diversity is, of course, difficult to define and measure and even more difficult to analyze is its impact on the cultural relevance of organizational practices and procedures. However, there is an inkling that apparently diverse organizations do have more contacts with and are more germane for minority populations.[106]

ORGANIZATIONAL CHANGE. The organizational literature, as motley as it is, expresses little doubt that bureaucratic models of organization, seemingly inevitable, stunt efforts to reach into minority communities or to attract minority clientele. As an example the failures of the community mental health organizations have frequently been laid at the feet of bureaucratization. The idea of those centers was to settle into those communities with serious needs (often minority and deprived communities) and to provide a range of services and, most importantly, involve the community in planning, program development, and service delivery. In a disturbing number of cases what occurred was the importing of a bureaucratic organization into a minority community, which in effect left it closer to the problem geographically, but still a stranger.[107] While many centers professed confusion over their implied roles as change agent and therapist, all too often the therapist won out, leaving the status of social change as facile rhetoric.[108] It was not evil intent gumming up the works here; it was the inability to imagine the organization in any other garb except bureaucratic. We must take seriously other ways of viewing organizations and, as appropriate, opt for change in what appear to be seemly directions. For instance Argyris' Model II of organizations is a likely new perspective. It calls for recognition of the organization, at its essence, as a mutual learning environment. It assumes that any organizational task or function over time requires learning — valid information, cooperation, openness, reduced interpersonal defensiveness, joint decision making and evaluation, as well as technical expertise — in order to be accomplished effectively and satisfyingly. It assumes, too, a double-loop learning process so that a client may learn from a worker and in like kind the worker may learn from the client and the administrator from both. That learning forms the energy for continual organizational change, and responsiveness is required by the external environment of service.[109]*

In reconsidering the organization the limits of technical expertise as the sole arbiter of intervention and goal attainment must be admitted. More important than the craft and cunning of the professional or the regularities and niceties of organizational structure is the understanding of the sociocultural context in which the intervention is conceived and offered — the microcosm of gesture, nuance, belief, ritual, and demeanor. In isolation the power of technology in the human services is vastly overrated. We have alluded to technologies seemingly as firm as those of public health crashing on the rubble of cultural ignorance. The same is no less true of behavioral methods and techniques.

One model, not without its problems of course, for this kind of organizational change is the community mental health center in East Los Angeles, an area that has one of the highest concentration of Hispanics in the United States. Karno and Morales have described the effort to create a center that would attract local residents and still perform basic mental health functions. Basically the design included all of the things we have mentioned above — the center eventually becoming a recognized and accepted part of the community and at the same time maintaining its professional mission and effectiveness.[110]

REVISING TECHNIQUES AND THEORIES OF INTERVENTION. We have previously indicated the limitations, culturally, of theories and techniques of intervention. Whether the effort is to reduce the abusive behavior of parents, to prepare a child for foster home placement, to counsel a distressed family, or to get teenagers off the street and into a job training program or school, it is guided by preconceptions, theories, and philosophies, all articulated through a bag of technical operations. One's preferences in this regard do not have to be junked, but they must be leavened by the yeast of cultural awareness.

To illustrate: to place a black child in a foster home because the mother can no longer support him or her financially and emotionally and to do so without understanding how to make use of the fosterage system may not only fail to mold methods to culture but snatch the child out of a comfortable and possibly secure environment and in

---

*We do not think, however, that Argyris intended his model to include the consumer in the learning cycle.

the end perhaps could create more emotional turmoil than one hopes to prevent.

Our family therapies, improvements as they may be, are founded on cultural preferences. Lidz' notions of the skewed and schismatic schizophrenogenic families may, generally, be full of truths. However, at the start it implies certain good and bad parental relationships and ideas that to an alarming extent turn on cultural regularities.[111] To employ mindlessly such a theory in helping a Hispanic family cope with a schizophrenic son (not to mention the possible bias in the definition of schizophrenic itself) may be an empty strategy if we do not understand the importance of compadrazgo, machismo, and *respecto* (respect of the other). Or to work only with the nuclear family when the weaknesses in the rest of the kinship system are critical for the fate of the child is to toil, probably, in failure. The son, enmeshed in the kin network, cannot be understood without understanding, too, the family's adjustment to stress.

Although even if we were not to alter and fill out theories of helping, the strategies we select to help may be critical for success. If a black family is disillusioned about the possibility of altering external (political, social, and economic) circumstances and if they cannot perceive the relevance of insight development or cathartic release, then the helper, no matter what the preference, may have to be more active and directive.[112]

As you might expect, or as every human service professional should know, establishing trust as a prelude to an effective helping is a critical initial process. Always difficult, under the best of circumstances, establishing trust is especially of the moment in cross-cultural helping efforts; the culturally different client must have a sense of assurance that his or her cultural integrity will not be violated or impertinently questioned. In that effort, the helping person can give the development of trust a push by honoring the importance of personalismo and dignidad and affective existentialism; getting to the business at hand must attend the creation of an interpersonal atmosphere of warmth, ease, and friendliness and gestural and verbal statements of recognition of, and respect for, the culture.

ASSESSING THE CULTURE. The novice or naive helping professional may at times mistake a cultural aberration for a legitimate cultural practice. Avoiding such a mistake requires adequate cultural learn-

ing as a prefatory step. The line between the accepted and normative behavioral expressions of culture is sometimes very difficult to
draw, and the worker, too, often toils in uncertainty or ignorance.
For example when does the presumed authority of the father meld
into cruelty toward a recalcitrant child? When do the elaborately
drawn delineations between male and female perquisites become an
occasion for the emotional oppression of the female? Flawed child-
rearing practices may become more obvious under the multiple tensions of discrimination and poverty, and the worker is drawn into
the necessity to make a judgment about physical discipline lapsing
into abuse.[113] A medley of such examples could be composed here.
The point is clear, however: Human service workers who are uninformed about the cultures upon which they encroach stand in constant jeopardy of perceiving pathology of deviance when, in fact,
they confront culture. Another problem related to the above tests the
ingenuity of helping professionals and paraprofessionals. What does
the individual do when a prescribed cultural practice is, by the
worker's most careful definition, problematic, even pathological? A
more difficult judgment obviously, but a rule of thumb might be: If
it is a genuine cultural practice and if the safety and health of an individual is not at stake, then the worker works around the integrity
of the culture and does not challenge it.

Culturally relevant practice in every human service area
demands a serious and far-reaching revision in our thinking about
the giving of help and the organization of that giving. With few exceptions the human service agency wanting to rework its practices
and policies to be more in tune with ethnic minority cultures will
have to do so from within. In this day and time, it is not likely to be
required by any external agency, except for occasional broad strokes
demanded by the courts or regulatory agencies. Helping others is
difficult enough under the best of circumstances; when it must be
done in a multicultural environment, it requires the best that we can
do.

SUMMARY

Child and family services, programs essential for the health and
welfare of our most precious human resource — children and their
families — have become a complex, confusing, and sometimes

redundant or deficient, network of agencies and policies. The liabilities of deprivation and racism and its attendant barriers lay a heavy burden on many of our minority families; yet many of the agencies that would serve these families fail them or worse yet add to that burden. Part of this failure is reasonably understood, we believe, as a misunderstanding (or lack of understanding) of the cultures, which form the backdrop against which these individuals act out their lives. To begin to change this situation requires at least the following:

1. revising and refurbishing some of our assumptions about helping families and children
2. learning about and appreciating elements of the other cultures and subcultures we serve so that we may flesh out our methods of assessment and helping
3. changing the organizational context of service (policy and program or structure and process) to create an environment more hospitable and responsive to cultural difference
4. recognizing the validity of other cultures and the critical importance of creating a culturally sensitive helping network

Anything less than these minima in a democratic and pluralistic society is simply inexcusable.

REFERENCES

1. This is only an approximation and is based primarily on the increase in working mothers (in two parent families) and the steady rise in solo parent families. *See* United States Department of Commerce, Census Bureau: *Population Profile of the United States, 1976;* U.S. Department of Commerce, Census Bureau: *Statistical Abstract of the United States, 1978.* Washington, D.C., U.S. Government Printing Office, 1978.
2. U.S. Department of Labor, Office of Policy, Planning, and Research: *The Negro Family: The Case for National Action.* Washington, D.C., U.S. Government Printing Office, 1965.
3. Staples, Robert: Towards a sociology of the Black family: A theoretical and methodological assessment. *Journal of Marriage and the Family, 33*:19-38, 1971.
4. Kadushin, Alfred: *Child Welfare Services.* 3rd. ed., New York, Macmillan, 1980, pp. 25-27.
5. Romanyshyn, John M.: *Social Welfare: From Charity to Justice.* New York, Random House/Council on Social Work Education, 1971, pp. 183-196.
6. Galper, Jeffrey H..: *The Politics of Social Services.* Englewood Cliffs, New Jersey, Prentice-Hall, 1975, pp. 28-30.
7. National Council of Organizations for Children and Youth: *America's Children, 1976.* Washington, D.C., National Council of Organizations for Children and

Youth, 1976, p. 22.

8. *Ibid.*, pp. 22-23.
9. Democratic Study Group: *Special Report: Gramm-Latta — What the House Adopted.* Washington, D.C., Democratic Study Group, July 2, 1981, pp. 17-18.
10. Cloward, Richard A., and Piven, Frances Fox: *Regulating the Poor: The Functions of Public Welfare.* New York, Random House, 1971. *See* epilogue.
11. Levy, Frank: *The Logic of Welfare Reform.* Washington, D.C., Urban Institute Press, 1980, p. 23.
12. *Ibid.*, pp. 27-30; Herzog, Elizabeth: *About the Poor.* Washington, D.C., Department of Health, Education, and Welfare, Social and Rehabilitation Services, Children's Bureau, 1967; Romanyshyn, *op. cit.*, pp. 231-232.
13. Kadushin, *op. cit.*, p. 79.
14. *Ibid.*, p. 80.
15. *Loc. cit.*
16. Beck, Dorothy Fahs, and Jones, Mary Ann: *Progress on Family Problems: A Nationwide Study of Clients' and Counselors' Views of Family Agency Services.* New York, Family Service Association of America, 1973, p. 22.
17. Lerner, Barbara: *Therapy in the Ghetto: Political Impotence and Personal Disintegration.* Baltimore, John Hopkins University Press, 1973; Goldberg, Carl, and Kane, Joyce D.: A missing component in mental health services to the urban poor: Services in-kind to others. In Evans, Dorothy A., and Claiborn, William L. (Eds.): *Mental Health Issues and the Urban Poor.* New York, Pergamon Press, 1974, pp. 91-110.
18. Lewis, Ronald G., and Ho, Man Keung: Social work with native Americans. *Social Work, 20*:379-382, 1975.
19. Stack, Carol B.: *All our Kin: Strategies of Survival in a Black Community.* New York, Harper and Row, 1974, Chapter 4.
20. Solomon, Barbara Bryant: *Black Empowerment: Social Work in Oppressed Communities.* New York, Columbia University Press, 1976, pp. 104-132.
21. Office of Federal Register, National Archives and Recordes Service, General Services Administration: *United States Government Manual.* Washington, D.C., U.S. Government Printing Office, revised May 1981, pp. 296-297.
22. *Ibid.*, p. 297.
23. *Ibid.*, p. 311.
24. Billingsley, Andrew, and Giovannoni, Jeanne M.: *Children of the Storm.* New York, Harcourt, Brace, and Jovanovich, 1972, pp. 80-85.
25. Ladner, Joyce A.: *Mixed Families: Adopting Across Racial Boundaries.* New York, Doubleday/Anchor, 1977; Jones, Charles E., and Elso, John F.: Racial and cultural issues in adoption. *Child Welfare, LVII*:373-382, 1979; McRoy, Ruth G.M.: *A Comparative Study of the Self-concept of Transracially and Uniracially Adopted Black Children.* Austin, Texas, University of Texas, Ph.D. dissertation, May, 1981.
26. Emlen, Arthur, et al.: *Barriers to Planning for Children in Foster Care.* Portland, Oregon, Portland State University, Regional Research Institute for Human Services, February, 1976; Pike, V.: Permanent planning for foster children:

The Oregon project. *Children Today,* 5:22-25, 41, 1976; Sisto, Grace W.: An agency design for permanency planning in foster care. *Child Welfare,* LIX:103-111, 1980.

27. Fanshel, David: Status changes of children in foster care: Final results of the Columbia University longitudinal study. *Child Welfare,* 143-171, 1976.

28. Rubenstein, Hiasura, and Bloch, Mary Henry (Eds.) *Things That Matter: Influences on Helping Relationships.* New York, Macmillan, 1982, pp. 277-280.

29. Gil, David: *Violence Against Children: Physical Abuse in the United States.* Cambridge, Harvard University Press, 1970; Gelles, Richard J.: Violence toward children in the United States. *American Journal of Orthopsychiatry, 48*:580-592, 1978; Reporting abuse and neglect. *Child Today,* 6:27-28, 1977.

30. Gil, *op. cit.;* Ryan, James H.: Child abuse among Blacks. *Sepia, 22*:227-230, 1973.

31. Feigelson, Naomi Chase: *A Child is Being Beaten: Violence Against Children, an American Tragedy.* New York, Holt, Rinehart, and Winston, 1975.

32. Erickson, Kai T: Notes on the sociology of deviance. In Becker, Howard (Ed.): *The Other Side.* Glencoe, Illinois, The Free Press, 1964, pp. 9-15; *see also* Erikson's fascinating study of this phenomenon: *The Wayward Puritans: A Study in the Sociology of Deviance.* New York, Wiley, 1966.

33. Myrdal, Gunnar: *An American Dilemma: The Negro Problem and Modern Democracy.* New York, Harper, 1944, pp. 1021-1026; Tocqueville, Alexis: *Democracy in America.* New York, Alfred A. Knopf, 1956, Vol. II, pp. 182-186.

34. Staples, Robert: Changes in the American and Afro-American family: Their implications for social and economic policy. *Proceedings of the National Conference of Catholic Bishops' Hearing on "The Family,"* Washington, D.C., 1976, pp. 4-9.

35. Murillo, Nathan: The Mexican-American family. In Hernandaz, Carrol A., Haug, Marsha J., and Wagner, Nathaniel (Eds): *Chicanos: Social and Psychological Perspectives.* St. Louis, C.V. Mosby, 1976, 2nd ed., pp. 15-17.

36. Lewis, Oscar: *The Study of Slum Culture — Background for 'La Vida.'* New York, Random House, 1968, one of the most complete statements of the "theory" of the culture of poverty; a slightly condensed version appears in the introduction to *La Vida.* New York, Random House, 1965, pp. xlii-lii.

37. Among many others, perhaps the most vocal critics of the idea were Robert Staples, Herbert Gans, and Andrew Billingsley.

38. Chestang, Leon: The delivery of child welfare services to minority group children and their families. In *Child Welfare Strategy in the Coming Years.* Washington, D.C., USDHEW pub. no. 18-30158, 1977, pp. 179-181.

39. Rodman, Hyman: Family and social pathology in the ghetto. *Science, August 23*:752-756, 1968.

40. *America's Children, op. cit.,* p. 23.

41. *Loc. cit.*

42. Geertz, Clifford: *The Interpretation of Culture: Selected Essays.* New York, Basic Books, 1973, pp. 15-17.

43. Ryan, William: *Blaming the Victim.* New York, Pantheon Books, 1971, pp. 130-142.

44. Meyer, James A.: Suburbia: A wasteland of disadvantage youth and negligent schools? In Bernard, Harold W., and Huckins, Wesley C. (Eds.): *Exploring*

Human Development: Interdisciplinary Reading. Boston, Allyn and Bacon, 1972, pp. 142-149.

45. *Ibid.,* p. 142.
46. Cottle, Thomas J.: *Black Children, White Dreams.* Boston, Houghton-Mifflin, 1974, p. 52.
47. *Ibid.,* p. 154.
48. *Loc. cit.*
49. Boulette, Teresa Ramirez: The Spanish speaking/surnamed poor. In *Child Welfare Strategy in the Coming Years.* Washington, D.C., DHEW pub. no. 18-30158, 1977, p. 405.
50. Montiel, Miguel: Social science myth of the Mexican American family. *El Grito, summer,* 1970.
51. Ruether, Rosemary Radford: Misogynism and virginal feminism. In Reuther, Rosemary Radford (Ed.): *Religion and Sexism.* New York, Simon and Schuster, 1974, pp. 1964-166.
52. Boulette, *loc. cit.;* Padilla, Amando M.: Psychological research and the Mexican American. In *La Causa Chicana: The Movement for Justice.* New York, Family Service Association of America, 1972. The point is made that almost *all* social scientists have accepted most *all* of the myths.
53. Ladner, Joyce A.: *Tomorrow's Tomorrow.* New York, Doubleday/Anchor, 1971, pp. 39-54.
54. Myers, Lena W.: *Black Women: Do They Cope Better?* Englewood Cliffs, New Jersey, Prentice-Hall, 1980, pp. 63-84.
55. Ladner, *op. cit.,* pp. 45-51.
56. Murray, Albert: *The Omni-Americans: New Perspectives on Black Experience and American Culture.* New York, Outerbridge and Dienstfrey, 1970, pp. 28-29.
57. *Ibid.,* p. 31.
58. Keefe, Susan Emly: Acculturation and the extended family among urban Mexican Americans. In Padilla, Amado M. (Ed.): *Acculturation Theory, Models, and Some New Findings.* Boulder, Colorado, Westview Press, 1980, pp. 85-110.
59. Dieppa, Ismael, and Montiel, Miguel: Hispanic families: An exploration. In Montiel, Miguel (Ed.): *Hispanic Families: Critical Issues for Policy and Programs in Human Services.* Washington, D.C., National Coalition for Hispanic Mental Health and Human Service Organizations, 1978, pp. 1-8.
60. Souflee, Frederico, Jr.: Biculturalism: An existential phenomenon. In Wright, Roosevelt, Jr. (Ed.): *Black/Chicano Elderly: Service Delivery in a Cultural Context.* Proceedings of the first annual Symposium on Black/Chicano Elderly, Arlington, Texas, The University of Texas at Arlington, 1980, pp. 21-23.
61. *Ibid.,* p. 27.
62. Frazier, E. Franklin: *The Negro Family in the United States.* Chicago, University of Chicago Press, 1966 ed.
63. Blauner, Robert: Negro culture: Myth or reality? In *Black Experience: The Transformation of Activism,* New Jersey, A Trans-Action publication, 1970.
64. Murray, *op. cit.,* pp. 48-54.
65. Gwaltney, John L.: *Drylongso: A Self-Portrait of Black Americans.* New York, Random House, 1980, p. xxvi.
66. Seelig, J.M.: *The Cultural Dimension in Learning and Child Development — New*

Policy Implications. New York, Institute on Pluralism and Group Identity, 1975, p. 2.

67. Shimkin, Demitri B., Shimkin, Edith M., and Frate, Dennis A. (Eds.): *The Extended Family in Black Society.* The Hague, Mouton, 1978, pp. 66-76.

68. Stack, *op. cit.,* pp. 62-74.

69. Martin, Elmer P., and Martin, Joanne Mitchell: *The Black Extended Family.* Chicago, University of Chicago Press, 1978, pp. 39-48.

70. Stack, *op. cit.,* p. 70.

71. *Ibid.,* pp. 62-67.

72. *Ibid.,* pp. 82-89.

73. Shimkin, *op. cit.,* pp. 76-86.

74. *Ibid.,* pp. 139-142.

75. *Loc. cit.*

76. Aschenbrenner, Joyce: Continuities and variations in Black family structure. In Shimkin, *op. cit.,* pp. 197-198.

77. *Ibid.,* pp. 181-200; *see also* Scanzoni, John H.: *The Black Family in Modern Society.* Chicago, University of Chicago Press, 1977, pp. 133-136.

78. Adams, Bert N.: Isolation, function, and beyond American kinship in the 1960s. *Journal of Marriage and the Family, 32:*592, 1970.

79. Boulette, *op. cit.,* p. 405.

80. Murillo, *loc. cit.;* for a more skeptical view of the Hispanic extended family *see* Ramos, Reyes: Am I who they say I am? In Trejo, Arnulfo D. (Ed.): *The Chicanos: As We See Ourselves.* Tucson, University of Arizona Press, 1979, pp. 60-61.

81. Schmidt, Fred H., and Koford, Kenneth: The economic condition of the Mexican-American. In Tyler, Gus (Ed.): *Mexican-Americans Tomorrow.* Albuquerque, University of New Mexico Press, 1975, pp. 92-98.

82. Baron, Augustine, Jr.: *The Utilization of Mental Health Services by Mexican-Americans: A Critical Analysis.* Palo Alto, R and E Research Associates, 1979, pp. 76-78.

83. Murillo, *op. cit.,* pp. 19-24.

84. LeVine, Elaine S., and Padilla, Amado M.: *Crossing Cultures in Therapy: Pluralistic Counseling for the Hispanic.* Monterey, California, Brooks/Cole, 1980, pp. 41-44.

85. *Loc. cit.*

86. Holtzman, Wayne, H. et al.: *Personality Development In Two Cultures: A Cross-Cultural Study of School Children in Mexico and the United States.* Austin, University of Texas Press, 1975.

87. *Ibid.,* p. 348.

88. Levine and Padilla, *op. cit.,* pp. 45-48.

89. Boulette, *op. cit.,* pp. 414-418.

90. Keefe, *op. cit.,* pp. 93-103.

91. Presthus, Robert: *The Organizational Society: An Analysis and a Theory.* New York, Vintage, 1965, pp. 14-25.

92. Baron, *op. cit.,* pp. 85-86.

93. Florez, John: Issues and problems affecting Hispanic youth: An analysis and a blueprint for action. In Montiel, *Hispanic* . . . *op. cit.,* pp. 76-78.

94. Argyris, Chris: Dangers in applying the results from experimental social pschology. *American Psychologist, April:* 481-482, 1975.

95. Finch, Wilbur A., Jr.: Social workers versus the bureaucracy. *Social Work, 21:*370-375, 1976; Ford, David C., Jr.: Cultural influences on organizational behavior. *Social Change, 8:*2-3, 1978; Rose, LaFrances: *The Dominant Values of Black Culture.* Princetown, New Jersey, Educational Testing Service, unpublished manuscript, 1972.

96. Christensen, Edward W.: Counseling Puerto Ricans: Some cultural considerations. In Atkinson, Donald R., Morten, George, and Sue, Derald Wing (Eds.): *Counseling American Minorities: A Cross-Cultural Perspective.* Dubuque, Wm. C. Brown, 1979, pp. 161-162.

97. Rose, *op.cit,* pp. 24-25; Christensen, *op. cit,* pp. 164-165.

98. Christensen, *op. cit.,* pp. 161, 166; Brosnan, Joan: A proposed diabetic educational program for Puerto Ricans in New York City. In Brink, Pamela J. (Ed.): *Transcultural Nursing: A Book of Readings.* Englewood Cliffs, New Jersey, Prentice-Hall, 1976, pp. 266-268.

99. Rose, *op. cit.,* pp. 26-27.

100. Levine and Padilla, *op. cit.,* pp. 190-192.

101. Leininger, Madeline: *Transcultural Nursing: Concepts, Theories, and Practices.* New York, Wiley, 1978, pp. 148-153; Leininger, Madeline (Ed.): *Transcultural Nursing.* New York, Masson International Nursing Publications, 1979, pp. 9-26.

102. Leininger, 1978, *op. cit.,* p. 149.

103. Quoted in Ornstein, Robert E.: *The Mind Field.* New York, Grossman, 1976, p. 31.

104. Hall, Edward T., and Whyte, William Foote: Intercultural communication: A guide for men of action. *Human Organization, 19:*5-12, 1960.

105. The East-West Center of the University of Hawaii produces a considerable literature on cross-cultural learning.

106. Kanter, Rosabeth Moss: *Men and Women of the Corporation.* New York, Basic Books, 1977, Chapters 8 and 10.

107. Panzetta, Anthony F.: *Community Mental Health: Myth and Reality.* Philadelphia, Lea and Febiger, 1971, pp. 17-20.

108. Dumont, Mathew: *The Absurd Healer.* New York, Science House, 1969.

109. Argyris, Chris, and Schön, Donald A.: *Theory in Practice: Increasing Professional Effectiveness.* San Francisco, Jossey-Bass, 1976.

110. Karno and Morales, *op. cit.*

111. Lidz, Theodore, et. al.: *Schizophrenia and the Family.* New York, International Universities Press, 1965.

112. Harper, Frederick D.: What counselors must know about the social sciences of Black Americans. *Social Work, 20:* 379-382, 1975.

113. Boulette, Teresa Ramirez: Parenting: Special needs of low-income Spanish-surnamed families. *Psychiatric Annals, 6:*95-107, 1977.

Chapter 6

THE TRANSCULTURAL PERSPECTIVE:
A REVIEW AND SYNTHESIS

THE delivery of human services is increasingly becoming an intercultural phenomenon as the American population becomes more aware of its pluralistic composition. Professionals who have socially sanctioned responsibilities for providing these services and who, for reasons discussed throughout this book, foist their own notions of right and wrong, good and bad, normal and abnormal, etc., onto persons who do not share their values, beliefs, and ideologies have through cultural naivete, cognitive rigidity, or misunderstanding become pawns of the dominant political, social, and economic systems.[1] It is extremely blasé and, more importantly, unprofessional if not down right unethical for service providers to ignore the ethnocentric outlook they frequently bring to the helping process.

Providing help to persons from other cultural groups can often ignite cultural sensitivities on the part of the participants in the helping process, particularly when they perceive that their cultural predispositions are being challenged as a result of the interaction. Perhaps it is fair to say that the provision of human services occurs in a social and organizational milieu that is differentiated and thus divided by such factors as race, ethnicity, culture, social class, and socially assigned roles. Providers of service who are unaware of these divisions and who are either unwilling or unable to accommodate to them are likely to encounter resistance from those they attempt to serve. Such resistance will generally manifest itself in feelings of hostility, overt or subtle threats, or unwillingness to cooperate in the helping process. Without the full cooperation of those needing and seeking help, service often means that providers intervene in lives under severe and sometimes impossible handicaps. Clients, recipients, patients, etc., must be understood within their own natural cultural environments. They must not be made to accommodate to the cultures of providers as a prerequisite to receiving the services they need.

The major objective of this book has been to help human service providers become aware of and sensitive to the singular importance of culture as it affects their ability to effectively and efficiently give service to culturally different clients. We have attempted to provide a framework, the transcultural perspective, that recognizes and tolerates cultural differences between providers of service and those they serve without either having to assimilate the other. We cannot overstate the case for adoption of the transcultural perspective, a theoretical frame of reference that conceptualizes the practical problems involved in helping diverse cultural groups. It provides, we think, a focal point for developing sensitivity to cultural-specific aspects in the helping process so that professionals can begin to deal more skillfully and effectively with clients who represent the enormous variety of cultures and subcultures that make up American society.

Income Maintenance Services

There has been a steady growth in the number of public welfare programs, in the number of persons receiving benefits from these programs, and in the cost of maintaining these programs since the passage of the Social Security Act in 1935. According to Spindler, the cost of public welfare has risen sharply and steadily approximately tenfold from $3 billion in 1935 to over $38 billion in 1975.[2] The Joint Economic Committee of the U.S. Congress has estimated that this nation spent in excess of $140 billion to support the social welfare system in fiscal 1975.[3] It is obvious that this country must seek ways and means to make public welfare programs more effective, efficient, and less costly.

As many social problems, for example increasing numbers with incomes below the poverty line, rising unemployment rates, higher costs for the basic necessities of life, higher health care costs, and relentless inflation and erosion of the dollar, worsen and continue to unravel the fabric of society, we can, in all probability, anticipate the need for a bigger welfare system in the future. Ironically, however, the current need for an expanded welfare system is occurring at a time when the country's political and economic decision makers are pursuing public policies that will reduce expenditures for basic welfare programs. For example the Omnibus Budget Reconcilation Act of 1981 authorizes budget cuts in many basic health, education, and welfare programs. The food stamp program will be cut $1.7 billion in fiscal 1982, $2 billion in 1983, and $2.3 billion in 1984; child nutrition programs will be cut by $1.5 billion in 1982; housing assistance programs will be cut (funding is authorized for 153,000 units in 1982, down from the 210,000 units authorized in 1981, and the maximum percentage of income that a tenant is required to pay for rent is to be increased from 25 percent to 30 percent); increases in federal Medicaid spending have been curtailed; and for 1982, $3.9 billion is authorized for CETA programs, a 51 percent reduction in funding from the 1981 level. In addition, federal expenditures for the Aid to Families with Dependent Children (AFDC) program have been reduced by $1 billion for fiscal 1982. The current federal administration headed by President Reagan has also approved a proposal to further reduce AFDC expenditures by another $1 billion in fiscal 1983. Other proposed changes in the program include compulsory *workfare* under which welfare recipients would have to work off their benefits (states now have the right to adopt workfare or not, as they choose), cutting off the parent's benefits when the child reaches sixteen years of age instead of eighteen; counting federal fuel assistance received by an AFDC family as income in determining benefits; counting military pay if the absent father is a soldier; and prorating shelter costs if the welfare family lives with another family.

The monumental changes taking place in the environment of the public welfare bureaucracy will alter the relationships between welfare officials and those they serve. The interactions between welfare workers and their clients will take on a less personal character, that is clients will be dealt with in impersonal, complicated, often esoteric, and increasingly in bureaucratic ways. As a result clients will need the knowledge and abilities to deal effectively with the bureaucracy. Moreover, as pointed out by Street and associates, they will also need great patience (as when welfare officials refuse to make appointments and keep recipients waiting interminably), high tolerance for rudeness and insult (as when indigent users of hospital emergency rooms find that no one even notices they are trying to ask questions), and a rare readiness to make their private lives public (as when one is questioned about one's sex life by a stranger in an open cubicle of a welfare office).[4]

Increasing bureaucratization of the public welfare organization will inevitably lead to a reduction in the level of humanitarianism (a humanistic conviction that workers can be more humane, more sensitive to themselves and to their clients, and more caring for those who are deprived and whose needs are great) exhibited by its many employees. No longer will humanism be a primary goal in the relationship between the workers and their clients. Thus, the major challenge for public welfare workers today is to maintain their compassion in a dehumanizing system. Workers have a responsibility to bring caring back to welfare work.[5] But how can this be done? One way, in part, is for welfare workers to become responsive to the cultural differences of the clients they serve.

The cultures of public welfare organizations and the cultures of welfare workers (who, in most instances, are white and middle class) are often incongruent with the diverse cultures of minority group clients. For example the culture of many minority groups reinforces such practices as giving, borrowing, and lending money, goods, and services in a free manner, moving about in flexible (often crowded) living arrangements as changing circumstances require, and passing children back and forth among close and distant relatives as various persons find and lose work. Yet, many of these practices are formally proscribed by both the welfare bureaucracy and its employees mainly because of their middle-class, Anglo, cultural predispositions.[6]

Insensitivity to the cultural characteristics of clients is not only dehumanizing and degrading to them, but it also inhibits rather than facilitates the effectiveness of public welfare services. For example culturally insensitive workers will attempt to provide services to clients as if they are all alike. Race, ethnicity, and cultural backgrounds are not seen as integral parts of the client's personality and life history. As a result, the relationships between the workers and clients may curtail the chances for positive behavioral change. In addition clients will view services rendered as culture-bound, for example services guided by middle class, Anglo-Caucasian values in the defining of problems as well as of solutions, and irrelevant to their needs.

Blindness to the cultural predispositions of clients is further exacerbated when the organizations in which welfare workers work suffer from the pathologies of bureaucracy, such as immersion in red tape, rules and regulations requiring the need to fill out endless forms, the need to provide numerous verification documents, complex client eligibility requirements that change regularly, high staff turnover and large caseloads, and the flowering of the bureaucratic personality to whom the means or procedures of the organization become ends in themselves.[7]

Thus if welfare workers are to revive a humanistic orientation in the welfare bureaucracy, they will at least need to increase their level of sensitivity and awareness of cultural differences between themselves and their clients. Moreover they must be conscious of their own cultural characteristics, i.e. their assumptions, values, beliefs, attitudes, and personal behaviors, as well as those of the organizations in which they work. Regardless of their level of training, workers can broaden their knowledge, understanding, and appreciation of cultural characteristics of minority groups and how these characteristics manifest themselves both in the adaptive efforts of clients and the helping process. We have suggested throughout this book that cultural factors influence perception, thinking, beliefs, attitudes, language, and nonverbal behaviors. When the cultures of persons in the helping process are quite different, there will be clashes of perceptions, meanings, interpretations, and responses. These cultural differences are responsible for major problems in the effective delivery of needed services. In light of this, it is important that welfare workers be encouraged to increase their cultural awareness. This can be accomplished, in part, by attending conferences and workshops providing knowledge about various minority groups, enrolling in classes on the cultures of minority groups, reading relevant cultural literature, communicating with minority group welfare workers about cultural issues, and living in subcultural environments whenever possible. These experiences can help welfare workers expand the range of their concerns, enhance their helping efforts and most of all grow as human beings.

Aging Services

A more conservative mood in American society in recent years has affected policies and services to the minority aged. The inflation rate in recent years has also affected the minority aged. The needs of the minority aged are considerable in health, mental health, housing, transportation, income, and a host of other areas at the very time that services are being cut and the minority aged population is growing.

The minority aged are expected to increase in size from approximately one-tenth of the elderly population today to approximately one-sixth of the elderly population in the year 2035. The lack of good, reliable census data on the minority aged has compounded problems for policymakers and for everyone alike. What can be gleaned from the census data is not heartening. The early U.S. Bureau of the Census estimates derived from the 1980 Census were that of the total elderly population over age sixty-five, 13.6 percent of whites were below the poverty level, while 30.8 percent of Hispanics and 38.1 percent of blacks were below the poverty level.

Social Security, a program that has experienced considerable financial problems in recent years, is the most widespread program serving the minority aged. Many minorities have either not applied for Social Security, were never enrolled, were ineligible to enroll, or perhaps were reluctant to encounter the long arm of bureaucracy (some of these reasons apply in various ways as well to minority participation in Medicaid and Medicare).

The double-jeopardy thesis states that the minority aged suffer a kind of double jeopardy in being both minority and aged. This thesis has been the subject of considerable discussion in recent years and has been expanded by some to include other jeopardies, such as sex, handicapping conditions, and social class. There has been an increasing attention given the question of social class. Race and racism are immensely important, but so is social class and class factors in attempting to explain causative factors for oppression and exploitation of the minority aged.

The minority aged live in a world of organizations. Many social service organizations serving the minority aged, such as senior citizen centers, have made considerable strides in recent years in becoming culture-conscious. Still, many have a long way to go in this respect. Human service organizations serving the minority aged have increased their number of minority employees, but many more are needed. The overall complexion of policymaking, planning, and implementation in the area of aging is predominantly that of a certain race, sex, and social class as well. White, middle-to upper-class males predominate in Congress, in the Administration on Aging, in state departments on aging, and on down. White females are more heavily represented at the direct service level, with minority females and some minority males making some inroads.

The bureaucratic nature of human service organizations thwarts many minority aged. Language difficulties are a particular problem for many Hispanic aged and for other minority aged as well. Bureaucratic Spanish is often of not much more help to the Hispanic aged than if the forms explaining the service or program were in English. Almost by nature social service bureaucracies are not as responsive as they could be to the particular needs of the minority aged, for they have a seeming legal and social mandate to treat everyone the same, and yet everyone is not the same. Indeed, there is no sameness within even one minority group category: There are 288 North American Indian tribes, several different subgroups of Asian Americans, and different subgroups of Hispanics and blacks. Unfortunately, even many minority professionals working in bureaucratic organizations become adapted to a prevailing bureaucratic ethos that works against culture-conscious policies and programs.

The political context in which the minority aged find themselves in the 1980s in American society is critical. Two current political developments are particularly crucial: a movement of social policy decisions back to the states and local areas and overall budgetary cutbacks and limitations in social programs and social policies. Political action and advocacy for the minority aged will probably be most effective in the future at the local and state level. Knowledge of the general voting record of a local elected official is important, so too are analyses of the important issues affecting the minority aged and actions toward changes in policies and programs that affect the minority aged. Involvement in political parties and advocacy groups can help effect change. The human service organizations serving the minority aged need the actions of change agents as well. The minority aged need a *say* with respect to the policies and programs that affect them. Active citizen participation is a good place to start. The societal learning approach, whereby citizen participant and planner sit down to learn and plan together, is a most useful perspective. Change agents can work on a number of important problems; transportation is a particularly outstanding one. Better research is needed, both qualitative and quantitative, on the minority aged.

Despite some available services, the income of the minority aged remains at a very low level. Income inequality is an obvious and sad reality of life for the minority aged. Income equalization must be a first starting point for any comprehensive change effort on behalf of the minority aged. A commitment to income and social *security* for the minority aged can only ultimately be achieved when society (or at least sizeable segments of society) is oriented to equalitarian ends. Yet this societal commitment to equalitarian ends must be conjoined with a requisite degree or amount of economic productivity in society. Those societies which have the most advanced and comprehensive social services (Sweden and West Germany as examples) also have high degrees of economic productivity. However, a concern with economic *productivity* must as well be conjoined with a concern for economic *democracy*. There has not been quite as much discussion in recent years of broad-based ideological stances or movements (socialism for example) as with democratizing capitalism (and socialism). Social change efforts have taken a democratic turn (Solidarity in Poland and the increasing concern with economic democracy among some quarters in the United States). Democratic involvement of minority workers in decision making can be crucial in helping to ensure a better present and future for minorities. Democratic involvement of the minority aged who are outside of the work force in human service organizations and other organizations can help to do the same.

Aging policies and services that are oriented in a transcultural direction are designed in such a way as to recognize and respond to cultural differences. Social policies and programs serving the aged are faced with a question that is posed in other policy areas as well, namely, Can social policies and programs really be attuned to *differences*? Can social policies and programs achieve a certain degree of universalism and yet be pluralistic as well? Social policies, programs, and institutions serving the minority aged need to be as intricately tuned, particular, and change-conscious as the complex cultures of the minority aged they are designed to serve. Policies, programs, and institutions serving the minority aged need to be cross-culturally and anthropologically oriented and informed to even begin to encounter the considerable complexity of minority aging cultures on an equal footing.

Health and Mental Health Services

The medical establishment has been persistently and durably inured to cultural difference in the understanding of illness and in the provision of all kinds of medical care. Science is science, we are told. The need to understand the place of herbal medicine in the Hispanic community or to appreciate the importance of *susto* in the lexicon of sickness is a job for the anthropologist, not the physician or his supporting cast. Yet we know, or at least strongly suspect, that in order to provide substantial and effective medical care to many groups in this country we must understand the cultural dimensions of illness and healing. If we do not, then no matter how slick our technology or potent our knowledge, our help will always be less than it might be.

There is irony here. Under the pressure of inflation, the general conservative philosophy afoot in the land, the serious needs of the disadvantaged, and the discriminated against creep away from our consciousness. As this happens, such groups, often culturally different, will be forced back onto their own resources and ingenuity. This may encourage a significant growth of culturally specific alternative health care systems. Thus the tension and misunderstanding between the official medical enterprise and cultural health systems is sure to grow; however, it should not. Without question the provision of essential health care for all citizens must be built on mutual understanding, but at this point the situation does not seem promising for some sort of détente in this area.

Culture influences health and health care in a variety of ways. It probably has an effect, along with poverty, class, and geographical location, on access to medical services and thus is implicated in the relative health status of different groups. As we have noted several times throughout this book, culture is also the material out of which we forge our identity and part of our identity is our body image, sense of well-being, and the perception of our health, relative to some social norm. Thus, culture plays an indirect role in the degree of health "felt" by a given individual. Most importantly different cultures have different taxonomies of illness and different technologies of healing. In a pluralistic society like America many of these cultural systems have become eroded by the dominant views or exist in uncomfortable juxtaposition with the prevailing institutions, but they do exist, and for many ethnic minorities of color they are critical in defining what ails them and suggesting what acceptable treatment is available. These cultural definitions and perceptions of illness and healing are a part of other cultural systems — religion, family, language, etc. — and not oddities to tweak the interest of the social worker or visiting nurse. Finally, culture affects how individuals perceive and respond to pain and illness and thus is a factor in the effect of medication and direct intervention upon individuals.

Cultural differences about health and illness may, among other things, add up to differences in the incidence and prevalence of certain illnesses or the health status of groups and differences in the use of medical services, both cultural and normative, by various groups. The fact that blacks generally have a higher incidence and prevalence of essential hypertension and do not make full use of available pharmacology may have genetic and social meaning, but it is also related to cultural factors, some directly pertinent to health and others not.

Ethnic medical systems, contrary to popular notions, are well defined (even if some Hispanics do not use a curandero, most know what role the curandero plays and what sort of intervention can be expected within the province of curanderismo). Hispanics have culturally defined, behaviorally specific rituals for preparing herbal mixtures, role definitions for the folk healer, and instructions for the maintenance of *botanicas*. Black Americans have systems of witchcraft, rootwork, and spiritual curing. Native Americans have articulated symbolic systems dealing with the management of evils and the themes of death and rebirth. It is not known, and there is great debate about to what extent members of a given ethnic group make use of such systems. It is probable that as a person becomes upwardly mobile and as established medical care is available, alternative systems may diminish in importance. Their strength may also be related to generational membership and perhaps, too, to urban/rural orientation. We make no claim here to know the extent of the cultural medical enterprise. However, we do know it is important, at the least as a part of a prevailing cultural world view and at the most as an alternative or supplemental system of health and mental health care.

To get medical care to people and to make it efficacious when it gets there, the professions and functionaries of the medical establishment must not only understand and appreciate the cultural system but be prepared to use it as an adjunct or to fit their own practice around it as much as possible. To ignore it or revile it is to insult the culture and perhaps not give the scope of care that might otherwise be tendered.

It may be then that the folk healer has diminished in importance in ethnic cultures, but it is true that the understanding of illness, healing, the perception of cause and effect, and the response to both disease and ministration continues to be an important element of many cultures and subcultures, and it varies among them.

Family and Children Services

In no other area — being and becoming families and raising children — is culture more deeply implicated. The day-to-day intimacy, the care and feeding of growing human beings, the transformations and rituals of growth and change, and the press of the social worlds outside the family all demand a blueprint for action and a palpable sense of continuity and meaning. Culture provides that and more. It is through the family that culture first seeps into individual consciousness. It is in the family that the groundwork is laid for participation in the social worlds to come and the meeting of the biological and social requisites of human experience (play and work, learning and adaptation, orientation in time and space, etc.). The ways that we are family are in large measure prescribed by culture. In spite of these facts, in this country this polyglot blend of dialects and differences, cultures and subcultures, classes and ethnic groupings, and our understanding and treatment of families is embarrassingly lacking in cultural awareness and appreciation. We as professionals and citizens sometimes act as if there were only one way to be a family and as if all other ways are aberrations to be treated or changed. To provide an adequate social, political, and economic function for families in this country, many things will be required, and generations may pass before they are realized. Not the least of these requisites was implied by Margaret Mead in 1935. Her plea is even more urgent today: "If we are to achieve a richer culture, rich in contrasting values, we must recognize the whole gamut of human potentialities, and so weave a less arbitrary social fabric, one in which each diverse human gift will find a fitting place."[8] The human potentialities of which she speaks begin, of course, in biology, but they are articulated through culture. Her hope that we might honor cultural diversity seems very little closer to reality than when she wrote forty-five years ago. The political context of the 1980s, as the decade approaches its midpoint, seems feistily concerned with recreating the illusion of a cultural monolith.

The irony of our implacable insensitivity to the many cultures within our borders and of our notion of the "ideal" family is that family life is changing for us all. Many kinds of families exist in many forms, and they assume many functions. Working husband, domestic wife, and school-going children are only a reality for a small percentage of us. Yet our thinking about a family and the policies about, programs for, and services to a family seem predicated on the assumption that this is not only the norm but a working goal.

Black and Hispanic families, especially in low-income brackets, face extraordinary daily pressures, pressures that cry for a range of services and supports. These, however, are not abundant and in many cases are not germane. The problem for minority families in trouble is threefold:

1. Needed supports and services are inaccessible.
2. Needed supports and services do not exist.
3. The organization and provision of services and supports is culturally irrelevant or antagonistic.

This book has been addressed to the last problem, cultural access, for the most part.

Cultural insensitivity flows from different sources. The prevailing myth that minority families are a hodgepodge of individual and social pathology subverts adequate helping. Support and socialization become superseded by social control measures. Other myths, as extensions and distortions of cultural truths, the case of machismo for example, do their part to thwart competent assessment and intervention. Certainly racism, both institutional and individual, continues to corrupt helping. More to the point, such racism is often the beating heart of the myths and misrepresentations that erode our ability to understand others different from us.

Organizational philosophy and culture tend to be bound to the dominant culture and, therefore, too narrow. The interpersonal distance and detachment required by technology (professional intervention) and good bureaucratic practice frequently run counter to minority cultural preferences and expectations. Thus minorities of color who seek help find themselves in an organizational environment of ambivalence: On the one hand, its atmosphere bespeaks service; on the other, the atmosphere is alien, even hostile.

But the sturdiest roadblock to culturally pertinent service is sheer ignorance. We know the myths; they are reinforced every day for us through the media, ethnic jokes, day-to-day civil traffic, and official documents and pronouncements. However, it seems that we do not know the truth and are not enthusiastic about taking the steps to discover it.

To appreciate and understand another culture's version of family is one thing; to turn it into organizational policies and practices is quite another; it is not easy, but it can be done. As an example let us take the practice of fosterage prevalent in many black communities. For those helpers who happen to discover it, it is assumed too often to be an aberration, certainly a practice running against the best interests of the child. But understood as a logical outgrowth of a central cultural phenomenon, the extended family, it begins to make great sense (in terms of survival and socialization), much more so perhaps than a juridically proper fosterage. Consider, too, that a jural procedure making a black child a ward of the court is very likely to end in institutional placement for that child. In many cases what the child then faces is little more than incarceration and sequestering. Against such a backdrop, fosterage should be understood as a viable and legitimate family practice and resource, not a blight upon family life. However to understand fosterage and to be able to distinguish it from simply getting rid of a child, we have to know the culture.

A stance that many helping agencies take then is that other sociocultural systems are deviant or unhealthy and that individuals and families are somehow trapped in this bog of pathology. Given that the ideal is to change the system, both structurally and culturally. However, that must await broad political strokes; so the strategy inevitably requires changing the individual, and that boils down to wrenching the individual from the culture and family.[9] In recent years black and Hispanic leaders have become vocal about preserving their sociocultural systems because they understand that to set individuals and families adrift from their culture is to create marginal and alienated people. This belief in cultural integrity has spawned human service agencies controlled and administered by minorities for their people, but such an effort will never be enough. Majority-dominated institutions must learn to share their power and responsibility and to create pluralistic environments of helping and care.

A culturally sensitive organizational environment is a product of many changes and shifts in thinking and practice. First among these is cultural learning, a vigorous effort that goes far beyond the usual fascination with cultural exotica and is founded upon a clear-eyed conception of a given sociocultural system — its values, norms, patterns of relationship, socialization and control practices, and the like. Contact is a key here. Didactic learning will not suffice. In the end, the human service organization must reach out, touch, and incorporate the textures and fabric of the culture. This in turn can only happen if our view of organization and profession expands. The assumptions underlying both are ethnocentric, and they are scientific and technological in flavor oriented to doing, fixing, or, in Goffman's words, *tinkering* — bring your body or mind to us and we will repair it. On the other hand, some of the values of minority cultures are oriented to being, the quality of experience, and the meaning of experience. Speaking metaphorically, the human service organization must be as a whole brain, bilaterally symmetrical and operating out of both hemispheres, one capable of logic, analysis, order, and classification, the other adept at intuition, spontaneous comprehension, and holistic grasp.

Until human service organizations understand James Michener's caution about intercultural contact, the situation for minority families and their children will continue to be difficult. "If you reject the food, ignore the customs, fear the religion and avoid the people, you might better stay home; you are like a pebble thrown into the water; you become wet on the surface but you are never a part of the water."[10]

SUMMARY

Years ago, Charles Silberman wrote, ". . . the failure of the enormous American social welfare effort stems from the same factor that has produced the political strain between Negroes and white liberals: the social workers' preoccupation with doing *for* people instead of doing *with* them — a preoccupation that destroys the dignity and arouses the hostility of the people who are supposed to be helped. All too often, social services are motivated by a sense of superiority, a patronizing "white man's burden," an attitude that would offend the most thick-skinned slum dweller."[11] Things have not changed much, have they?

It has been our thesis that one part of this white-supremacy insinuation is ignorance of the culture of ethnic minority clients, a failing that makes service, when provided, less effective than it might be and in the extreme makes service inaccessible symbolically to those who may need it desperately. This insensitivity and this colonial patronage lies deep in the marrow of service organizations and their functionaries. As a result, encounters between service providers and clients are sometimes tense and hostile, unproductive and ineffective.

We have advocated a different perspective, a change of heart that demands rigor and devotion to accomplish so that service organizations can deftly and sensitively reach out to members of other cultures and incorporate their views and concerns into the whole cloth of service provision. We understand, of course, that such a perspective, a transcultural one, is merely a beginning and that many of its principal elements may be subject to challenge and debate. That is to the good. However, our point is that the effort must start if we are to begin to meet the legitimate needs and entitlements of thousands upon thousands of our citizens. To give people a sense of dignity that allows them to accept help and make use of it demands that we respect them as full humans in the best democratic tradition. To do that we must begin by respecting their culture.

REFERENCES

1. Pederson, Paul, Lonner, Walter J., and Draguns, Juris G.: *Counseling Across Cultures*. Honolulu, The University of Hawaii Press, 1976, p. vii.
2. Spindler, Arthur: *Public Welfare*. New York, Human Sciences Press, 1979.
3. Subcommittee on Fiscal Policy of the Joint Economic Committee of the United States Congress: *Handbook of Public Income Transfer Programs*. Studies in public welfare. Paper no. 20, Washington, D.C., Government Printing Office, 1975.
4. Street, David, Martin, George T., and Gordon, Laura K.: *The Welfare Industry*. Beverly Hills, Sage Publications, 1979, pp. 68-69.

5. Horejsi, John E., Walz, Thomas, and Connally, Patrick R.: *Working in Welfare: Survival Through Positive Action.* Iowa City, University of Iowa School of Social Work, 1977.

6. Street et al., *op. cit.,* p. 69.

7. Merton, Robert K.: *Social Theory and Social Structure.* New York, The Free Press, 1957.

8. Mead, Margaret: *Sex and Temperament in Three Primitive Societies.* New York, 1935, p.322.

9. Leininger, Madeline M.: *Nursing and Anthropology: Two Worlds to Blend.* New York, John Wiley and Sons, 1970, pp. 159-160.

10. Michener, James: *Reader's Digest, 106*:633, 1975. Quoted in Steffen, Mari L., and Francis, Joanne: Transcultural nursing experiences and care with migrant children. In Leininger, Madeline: *Transcultural Nursing: Concepts, Theories, and Practices.* New York, John Wiley and Sons, 1978, p. 293.

11. Silberman, Charles E.: *Crisis in Black and White.* New York, Vintage, 1964, p. 313.

INDEX

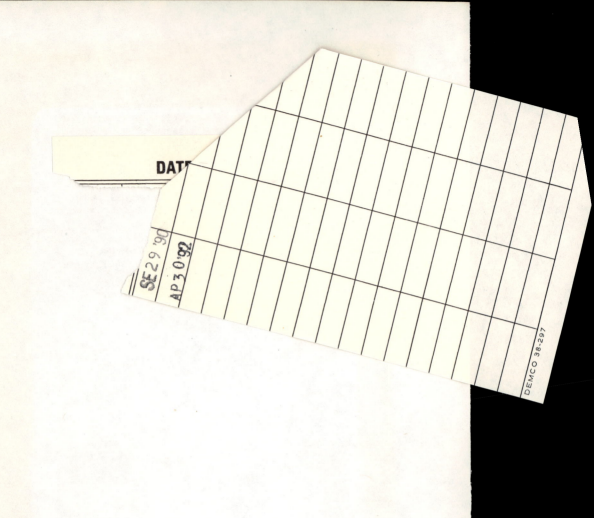